This simple guidebook provides YOU, the reader, with 8 Chapters full of information that will enable you to become a better contract negotiator. You will understand and learn about how to properly fact find, plan, and conduct a negotiation, and bargain for a better pricing arrangement using this text, and the Slides for this guidebook can be purchased directly from me by email me at the email address at WWW.ACQUISITIONINSTITUTE.NET.

If after read the guidebook, you would like the author, Mr. Robert K. Knauer, CPCM CPPO, to come and deliver training on the subject of contract negotiations, please contact him directly at (202) 280-7272. Information about Mr. Knauer and his offeriings is available at the following link which can be found at: WWW.ACQUISITIONINSTITUTE.NET, or simply "Google" Robert Knauer CPCM CPPO for more info.

Mr. Robert Knauer has been actively performing contract negotiations since 1984, after he'd left the U.S. Navy as a Lieutenant in the Supply Corps to become a GS-9 at the Navy Regional Contracting Office in Norfolk, Virginia. Since that time he worked his way from GS-9 to GS-14 in the federal government, moving from Norfolk and ultimately to Washington, D.C., where he became a senior contracting officer and negotiator for DOD, Treasury, Department of Labor, Department of Transportation (DOT), and professor of contract management where he developed and taught this course and several others for the Defense Acquisition University (DAU).

CHAPTER 1: INTRODUCTION TO NEGOTIATION

Learning Objectives

At the end of this chapter you will be able to:

Primary Learning Objective (PLO)
Describe general negotiation concepts.

Classroom Learning Objective 1/1
Describe the meaning of negotiation.

Classroom Learning Objective 1/2
Identify success factors and possible outcomes of the negotiation process.

Classroom Learning Objective 1/3
Describe the overriding negotiation themes.

Contents and Procedures

Chapter
Contents

In this chapter you will learn:

1.0 Chapter Overview

Introduction to
Negotiations

Negotiations is a part of everyday life. Many experts on the subject Say that life is one long negotiation. But, many readers feel that they are personally not experienced enough when I ask, "Who has had some experience negotiating a contract?" Since normally only a few hands go up, they feel they don't have experience negotiating, when in fact, they have probably negotiated many contracts both orally and made agreements which involve exchange of non-monetary considerations.

Since the use of negotiation skills is not limited to just government contracts, the first step to improve your own bargaining skill is to realize that you already have considerable experience negotiating agreements. Why? You negotiate with your spouse, your superior, subordinates, co-workers, friends all of the time. In fact, you are constantly bargaining with other people to fulfill both monetary and non-monetary needs.

Even with the nation's current financial crisis, there are many things you can negotiate better, cheaper, and obtain more value just by asking the right questions, or demanding a better price!

It has been said that, "We have to negotiate for everything we want in life." This is true, whether it be a job, marriage, a car, time off to play. So in other words, negotiation can be avoided only when we have no desire for something that someone else has. Because of this, everything we learn during this negotiation course can help YOU reach your personal and professional goals by improving your ability to negotiate successfully.

Government
Contract Negotiations

The Federal Acquisition regulation (FAR) establishes general procedures for contract negotiations between Government and industry in FAR Part 15. For the purposes of this course, negotiation means:

"Contracting through the use of either competitive or non-competitive proposals and conducting discussions. Any contract awarded without using sealed bidding procedures is considered a negotiated contract."

Generally the FAR describes negotiation as:

"A procedure that includes the receipt of proposals from offerors, permits bargaining (discussions), and usually affords offerors an opportunity to revise their submitted offers before contract award. Bargaining in the sense of discussion, persuasion, alteration of initial assumptions and positions, give-and-take, may apply to price, schedule, technical requirements type of contract (methods), or other terms and conditions of a proposed contract."

The FAR defines the term "discussion" to mean, "any oral or written communication between the government and an offeror, other than those required for clarification, whether or not initiated by the government that (a) involves

Information essential for determining the acceptability of a contractor's proposal or (b) provides the offeror with an opportunity to revise or modify its proposal."

The term, "offeror" instead of "contractor" is used by the Federal Government to refer to a third party in government contract negotiations. The use of "offeror" is correct because a "contract" does not and cannot exist until the negotiations conclude and the contractual terms are agreed upon in writing by both sides. This student textbook will use the term "contractor" instead of "offeror" because government contracting specialist often use the term "contractor" when referring to the other party in government contract negotiations.

For the purpose of this course and this book, the term "discussion" shall encompass both "fact-finding" (Chapter 2), "bargaining" or "negotiation" sessions in a non-competitive environment (Chapters 3, 4 and 9), and "competitive discussions" (Chapter 8).

1.1 The Negotiation Process

Description of Negotiation

Negotiation is a process of communication by which two parties, each with its own viewpoints and objectives, attempt to reach a mutually satisfactory agreement on, or settlement of, a matter of common concern.

The "mutually satisfactory agreement" in the end can be satisfactory to both parties only when the differences of viewpoints have been discussed and there is a meeting of the minds as well as acceptance of the viewpoints by both sides. However, it must be understood that negotiation is not a process of mutual sacrifice for the sake of agreement. Rather, it is a process of finding ways whereby both parties will have their interests maximized. It should also be understood that negotiation is not the same as "dictation," where one side imposes terms on the other side.

There is something special about the ambivalent relationships of the parties who negotiate in an attempt to reach an agreement: They are dependent on each other and yet have opposing interests. Labor and management, for example, cannot produce without each other. Likewise, buyers and sellers need each other to transact business. Whether in government or in business, people and organizations gain by making agreements.

To obtain agreement you must generally yield something in order to get something in return. In other words, "you have to give to get." As long as the gain you anticipate from the agreement is greater than the cost of what you would yield, you must be willing to yield and obtain agreement. The limit on yielding is reached when one or the other party believes that to yield more would be more costly than the gains from the agreement.

Success Factors In Negotiation

Successful negotiation — the achievement of an agreement that satisfies the best interests of your side — is a product of many factors. Factors that contribute to success in any negotiation always include:

- The specific circumstances surrounding each negotiation.

This may be viewed as the bargaining leverage available to each side. For example, the circumstances would generally favor the contractor if the government was bargaining for a high-demand product in short supply. Similarly, the circumstances favored General Schwarzkopf in the cease-fire negotiations he held with the defeated Iraqi generals after the Gulf War. After all, the Iraqi army had just taken a horrendous beating compared to the relatively minor losses of the allied coalition.

- **The bargaining skills of the negotiators.**

Highly skilled negotiators have greater opportunities for negotiation success than do negotiators who do not know how to bargain very well.

• The motivation and fairness of each party.

The greater the motivation and fairness on each side, the more likely it is that the negotiations will end in agreement. Conversely, the likelihood of successful negotiation decreases when either side is poorly motivated or unfair.

• The willingness of each party to make concessions.

Achieving successful negotiation becomes increasingly difficult when either side is unwilling to show any flexibility. **In contrast, successful outcomes become more likely when both parties are willing to yield and make concessions.**

Contract Bargaining Skills

To be an effective contract negotiator for the government, you need to acquire a number of skills that are taught in government courses. The following table outlines these skills and lists specific courses that enable negotiators to further develop contract bargaining skills:

Contract Skill	Course
Researching the requirement and the market for a particular product or service	Federal Acquisition Institute (FAI) "Procurement Planning" DoD "Management of Defense Acquisition Contracts Basic"
Applying policies and procedures for: • Soliciting • Awarding • Modifying contracts	FAI "Contract by Negotiation" FAI "Government Contract Administration" DoD "Management of Defense Acquisition Contracts Basic" DoD Intermediate Pricing Course
Analyzing costs and prices	FAI "Price Analysis" FAI "Cost Analysis" DoD "Principles of Contract Pricing"
• Factfinding • Preparation for negotiations • Conduct of negotiations • Bargaining techniques • Bargaining tactics • Nonverbal negotiating	You will learn these skills in this course

1.2 Negotiation Outcomes

**Outcomes/
Styles**

In general, there are three possible outcomes to every negotiation, depending on the long-term success or failure of each side. These outcomes are known as "Win/Lose," "Win/Win," and "Lose/Lose."

Two basic negotiation styles closely relate to the three different outcomes. There are win/win negotiators who strive for win/win outcomes, and there are win/lose negotiators who strive for win/lose and even lose/lose outcomes.

**Win/Lose
Outcomes**

When a negotiation results in a win/lose outcome, one side does significantly better than the other side and "wins," while the second party does poorly and "loses." The win/lose outcome is characterized in the framework where one side must lose in order for the other side to win. This type of negotiation tends to be highly competitive, with a large degree of mistrust on both sides.

Ironically, both sides often feel that they are the "losers" in a win/lose negotiation because of the rancor and mistrust that characterized the negotiation. Yet even the "losing" side might feel good at the conclusion of the win/lose bargaining session because of their immediate perception that they obtained the best deal possible under the circumstances. However, in the long run, the "losing" party often regrets the agreement after discovering that the deal wasn't so good after all. Consequently, the losing party becomes even more mistrustful of the other party and even more reluctant to continue a business relationship.

Win/lose outcomes often occur in one-time-only relationships involving private parties. Since neither party anticipates additional business beyond the initial transaction, there is no motivation to ensure long-term satisfaction for the other side. Examples of win/lose outcomes abound in everyday life, such as private home and auto sales where the bargainers generally do not have any more transactions with the other side.

In a "monopsony" situation, where the government is the only buyer, the government could achieve many short term wins to the detriment of contractors by "dictating" contract terms. But win/lose outcomes would have the following negative long-term consequences:

* Many suppliers on the losing end of win/lose government contracts would eventually be forced out of business.
* Other high-quality suppliers would no longer be willing to do business with the government
* There would be greater risk of poor-quality, overpriced deliverables from the remaining suppliers still willing to do business with the government.

Win/Win Outcomes

In contrast to the win/lose outcome, the win/win outcome is the scenario in which both sides achieve long-term satisfaction because each party feels that its side "won" and the "victory" was not at the expense of the other side. In a commercial relationship, each side has a vested interest in satisfying the long term goals of the other side. Any short term advantage achieved by wringing out every last concession is usually not as important as securing a long-lasting business relationship.

Win/win negotiations, also known as "both win" outcomes, are characterized by much higher levels of trust and cooperation. Win/win negotiations are also much less confrontational and contentious than the win/lose negotiations. Since each side expects to do business with the other side after the bargaining session is concluded, a primary negotiating goal of each party is the long-term satisfaction of the other side. Many bargaining sessions between commercial businesses are win/win negotiations because a win/lose outcome would jeopardize the long-term business relationship.

There are important reasons why government negotiators should strive for win/win outcomes. First, the Federal Acquisition Regulation (FAR) requires government contracting officials to obtain a price that is fair and reasonable to both sides. This requirement implies that the government should not "win" at the expense (or "loss") of the contractor. Secondly, the government has a vested interest in the long-term success and survival of government contractors. Not only are government contractors indispensable sources for products and services, but a win/win attitude enhances competition by encouraging more firms to do business with the government. In turn, increased competition reduces contract costs and improves quality. Moreover, well-stocked base of good-quality suppliers and vendors providing goods and services at reasonable prices is essential to the operations of the federal government.

Finally, win/win negotiators often achieve better outcomes because win/lose styles frequently result in demonstrations of similar tendencies by the other side. After all, who wants to be giving and trusting when the other negotiators display selfishness and mistrust. In contrast, the genuine concern demonstrated by win/win negotiators is, in turn, frequently reciprocated by the other party.

Lose/Lose Outcomes

A negotiating outcome where both sides lose is known as deadlock, or a lose/lose outcome. A deadlock occurs when final agreement cannot be obtained. Since both parties had a stake in a successful outcome of the bargaining session or they would not have been negotiating in the first place, both sides suffer a considerable loss when negotiations stalemate and deadlock occurs.

The contractor side loses more than just the profit projected on the lost government contract. The fixed costs associated with the contract must be absorbed by other business or contracts of the firm. This, in turn, either reduces company profit and may even contribute to overall company losses.

The fixed costs that would have been absorbed by the government contract, along with the profit associated with the contract, are known as contribution income. Besides losing contribution income, the contractor in a deadlock will not be paid for the direct costs that would have been associated with the government contract. The reduction in direct costs will often cause the contractor to lay off employees.

When a deadlock occurs, the government side also suffers a considerable loss because the desired deliverable or service often cannot be procured in a timely manner. This is particularly true when the government is negotiating with a single firm under an exception to "full and open competition." When deadlock occurs with a sole source contractor, the unique product or service cannot be obtained.

Sometimes, avoiding deadlock is very difficult when dealing with unfair or unyielding parties. The government negotiator must then decide on the better alternative: deadlocking or being on the losing end of a win/lose outcome. Nevertheless, considerable effort should be made to avoid a deadlocked negotiation because the government side will still suffer a significant loss.

The Importance of Perception in Determining Negotiation Outcome

Except for lose/lose outcomes, the perception of the result by each side determines whether an outcome is win/win or win/lose. In other words, the same contractual result could be viewed as being either win/win or win/lose depending on the "eyes of the beholder" or the perception of each side.

For example, a $100,000 contract price could be considered a win/win or win/lose outcome depending on how the contractor views that price. Since the government side should strive for win/win results, the perception of the contractor side becomes paramount. It is not enough for just the government to perceive a win/win outcome when the contractor side feels it was the victim of a win/lose result.

Because the other side's perception is so significant in determining negotiation outcomes, the negotiation style assumes utmost importance. The style or presentation is often the primary influence on the other side's perception. Regardless of the contract price, the contractor side is more likely to perceive win/win outcomes when the government exhibits win/win behavior. Conversely, the contractor side is more likely to perceive a win/lose result when the government side appears to have a win/lose attitude. Consequently, government negotiators should exercise great care in exhibiting the appropriate attitude or manner when negotiating.

Negotiation Styles

Win/lose styles can often be easily recognized because win/lose negotiators often give tell-tale signs that they are striving for this kind of result. Win/lose negotiators tend to be highly competitive and mistrustful of the other side. They are also generally argumentative and tend to focus on areas of disagreement. Another hallmark of win/lose bargainers is their reluctance to make any meaningful concessions. Since many win/lose negotiators are prone to deceptive behavior, they often resort to win/lose tactics and "gamesmanship" during the bargaining session.

In contrast to the win/lose style, negotiators exhibiting win/win styles are far more cooperative and trusting of the other side. Negotiators seeking win/win outcomes are more likely to make concessions when it is in the mutual interest. They tend to be more respectful of the other side, and attempt to seek agreement rather than to prove they are right and win arguments. Finally, win/win negotiators rely far less on deceptive behavior and, instead, focus on bargaining tactics that are win/win in orientation.

Spectrum of Negotiation Styles

Negotiation styles cover a wide range or spectrum because the behavior of negotiators is rarely either purely win/win or win/lose. Although government negotiators should conscientiously strive for pure win/win outcomes, many bargainers exhibit a combination of win/win and win/lose traits during the course of the negotiation.

For example, mildly mistrustful or deceptive behavior is sometimes exhibited by even the best win/win negotiators. The use of some win/lose traits may even be justified, particularly when dealing with win/lose negotiators on the other side. Similarly, win/lose negotiators often exhibit some win/win traits even though this behavior may be only intermittent or used as a ploy to deceive the other side.

The illustration below shows the two negotiation styles at each end. While the spectrum of styles ranges from 100 percent win/win to 100 percent win/lose, the overwhelming majority of negotiations styles fall somewhere between the two extremes.

```
win/win
  100%  90%  80%  70%  60%  50%  40%  30%  20%  10%  0%

  <--------------------------------------------------------------->

   0%   10%  20%  30%  40%  50%  60%  70%  80%  90%  100%
                                                     win/lose
```

Since the type of outcome is determined by the perception of the other side, there is no definitive point on the spectrum that can separate win/win from win/lose outcomes. For instance, government behavior that is 60 percent win/win and 40 percent win/lose may be considered win/lose by the contractor and could even result in deadlock. Likewise, there is always the possibility that a negotiating style that is 30 percent win/win and 70 percent win/lose may be perceived as a win/win outcome by the other side.

While the proportion of win/win behavior needed to produce win/win outcomes varies by negotiation and can never be known, the probability of a win/win outcome increases in proportion to the win/win behavior exhibited during the bargaining session. Conversely, the more win/lose behavior is used, the greater the likelihood of either win/lose or lose/lose outcomes.

Comparison of Negotiation Styles

The following table compares win/win and win/lose negotiation styles:

Outcome	Win/Win	Win/Lose
Negotiation Goal	Obtain agreement acceptable to both sides, including a fair and reasonable price	Obtain the best possible deal for your side regardless of consequences to the other side
Focus	Solve mutual problems	Defeat the other party
Environment	Cooperation and trust	Mistrust and gamesmanship
Negotiation Characteristics	• Resolve conflict • Obtain both short- and long-term satisfaction • Establish cordial, business-like relations • Combine efforts to satisfy the other side and solve problem	• Make extreme initial demands • Use deceptive ploys • Make stingy or no concessions • Attempt to win arguments instead of agreements

1.3 Overriding Negotiation Themes

Overriding Negotiation Themes

Government bargainers should always keep in mind the following overriding themes when negotiating government contracts:
- Think Win/Win
- Sell Your Position
- Win Agreements Instead of Arguments
- Everything Is Negotiable
- Make It Happen

Think Win/Win

Since win/win outcomes are preferred they are the paramount objective in government contract negotiations. Consequently government negotiators should consciously display win/win attitudes and negotiation styles. Most bargaining ploys and negotiation tactics should be avoided because these devices are deceptive in nature and generally give the other side the perception of win/lose negotiation style.

Sell Your Position

Negotiators are agents for the government trying to "sell" their positions to the other side. Accordingly, government bargainers should strive to be persuasive while being respectful and polite. In negotiations as in other forms of sales, it is easier to "sell" a product when the prospective customer likes and respects the salesperson.

Win Agreements Instead of Arguments

Negotiators should support their positions by winning *agreements* with the other side. Trying to "win the argument" is too often a sign of a win/lose negotiation. When argumentative behavior characterizes negotiations, one or both sides are likely to perceive a win/lose outcome even when the final agreement could otherwise appear balanced or fair. Remember that persuasion is not only a matter of logic and content, but also significantly depends on the manner of presentation.

Everything Is Negotiable

No negotiation position is sacred and off limits if it prevents the more important goal of a fair and reasonable settlement. Consequently, government negotiators must always be prepared to use common sense and be open to negotiate all issues.

Make It Happen

Negotiators as agents for their side are responsible for securing whatever their party needs from the other side by obtaining a negotiated settlement. To reach agreement, negotiators must often display creativity, initiative, and even courage. When the benefits of an agreement outweigh the costs, bargainers must somehow find a way to secure the deal and "make it happen!"

1.4 Chapter Summary

Summary

Since negotiation is a necessary part of everyday life, good bargaining skills are an asset for the individual as well as the government. Negotiation is basically a communications process where both sides try to reach a satisfactory agreement on issues of mutual interest.

The win/win outcome is the best of the three possible negotiation outcomes and should be the objective of every government negotiation. However, the type of outcome largely depends on the perception of each side. Consequently, the government's negotiation style is extremely important because it influences the perception of outcome type.

Government negotiators should always keep five overriding themes in mind during every negotiation:

- "Think Win/Win"
- "Sell Your Position"
- "Win Agreements Instead of Arguments"
- "Everything Is Negotiable"
- "Make It Happen"

CHAPTER 2: FACTFINDING

Learning Objectives

At the end of this chapter you will be able to:

Primary Learning Objective (PLO)
Describe the factfinding process.

Classroom Learning Objective 2/1
Identify types of information needed from contractors to complete analysis of the proposal. Seek any facts necessary to complete the analysis.

Classroom Learning Objective 2/2
Identify different methods of factfinding and selection criteria.

Classroom Learning Objective 2/3
Describe the process and guidelines for selecting and preparing government employees to participate in factfinding sessions with contractors.

Classroom Learning Objective 2/4
Describe the factfinding process.

Classroom Learning Objective 2/5
Describe the potential results of factfinding.

Contents and Procedures

Procedural Steps   The following flow chart outlines the steps of factfinding:

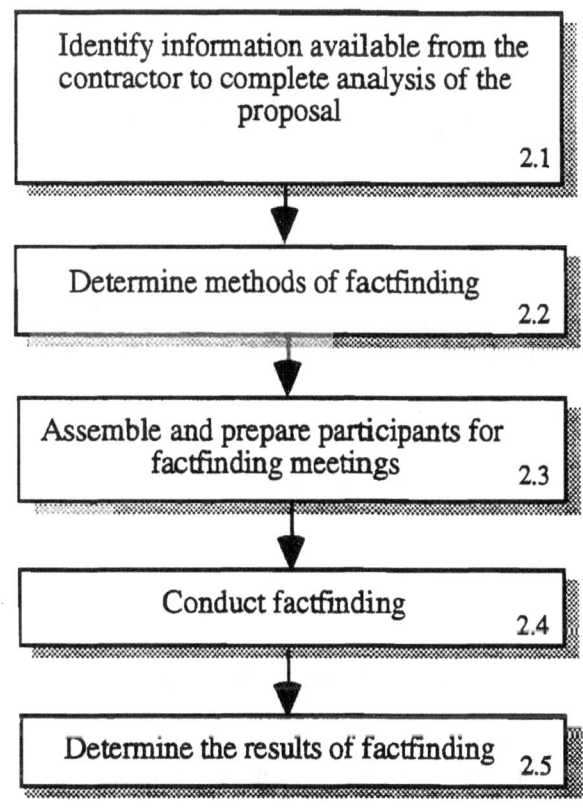

2.0 Chapter Overview

Necessary Information

The presentation in this chapter begins after completion of your initial analysis of the proposal. At this point, you should have in hand:

- The solicitation

- The proposal and all data submitted by the contractor to support the proposal

- Data from your research of the deliverable, the market for the deliverable, any relevant acquisition histories

- Any field pricing reports or audits

- Your analysis of the proposed price and, where appropriate, of the different cost elements

- Technical reviews

Define Factfinding

Factfinding is communication with the contractor (orally or in writing) to identify and obtain all information available from the contractor necessary to complete the analysis of the proposal. In addition, factfinding sessions provide the contractor with an opportunity to seek clarification of the government's stated requirements (including the statement of work and any other term or condition of the solicitation).

When Factfinding Is Necessary

The government may need to factfind when information submitted by the contractor appears to be incomplete, inconsistent, ambiguous, or otherwise questionable.

Purpose of Factfinding Sessions

The FAR represents "factfinding sessions with the offeror" as part of the process of establishing the government's negotiation objectives . To establish meaningful objectives prior to negotiation, both sides need a clear understanding of all the work to be performed under the contract and the terms and conditions that each has put on the table (the government in its solicitation, the contractor in its proposal). Hence, both parties should view factfinding as an opportunity to exchange information and clear up misunderstandings or erroneous assumptions that could impede the upcoming negotiation.

Types of Information Clarified	Factfinding centers on clarifying matters:
	
	• Affecting cost
	
	   For example:
	
	    - Data requirements
	    - Delivery schedule
	    - Design problems
	    - Production problems
	
	• Identifying assumptions
	
	   For example:
	
	    - The use of initial production lots in calculating learning curve slopes.
	    - Identification of which escalation index(es) will be applied and the time period for the index(es).

Distinguish Factfinding from Negotiation	During factfinding, there is often a strong temptation to immediately counter the contractor's position. However, factfinding is not the same as the bargaining session and to do so would destroy the purpose of the session. It is extremely important that both parties avoid any attempt to negotiate during a factfinding session. Factfinding is somewhat analogous to the discovery process in our legal system. Bargaining during the factfinding session causes the government side to lose in two ways. The negotiations may inadvertently harm the government position because the issues are negotiated before analysis is completed. Once negotiation begins, it becomes less likely that the remaining factfinding issues will be clarified.
When Factfinding Occurs	Factfinding before the negotiation conference permits the government negotiator to evaluate the facts, establish a negotiation objective, and get necessary clearances. For smaller, less complicated procurements with considerable historical data, the interval between stages is often short; sometimes the bargaining even occurs on the same day, immediately after the factfinding session. Larger, more complicated procurements generally require a lengthy break between factfinding and negotiation session to give both sides sufficient time to digest the acquired information. Another reason for a delay is to give both sides enough time to submit an updated solicitation or proposal. Factfinding does not always end when negotiations begin. Questions and clarifications are generally a continuing process throughout the negotiation, particularly clarifications in the statement of work, product description, and contract specifications. Factfinding continues to serve the important purpose of assuring mutual understanding before an issue is negotiated.

2.1 Identify Information Available from the Contractor Necessary to Complete Analysis of the Proposal

Focus of Factfinding

Factfinding closely follows the first analysis of an offer, which raises questions and discloses apparent inconsistencies and areas that need to be explored in more detail.

The government side looks for two kinds of facts when cost analysis is required:

- First, establish the actual costs of doing the same kinds of tasks. This determination is then used as a bench mark against which to measure the probable future costs of the upcoming contract.

- Second, isolate the assumptions and judgments made by the contractor in getting from the indicated current costs to probable future costs.

2.2 Determine Methods of Factfinding

Factfinding in Typical Contracting Situations

The following table outlines appropriate methods of factfinding in typical contracting situations:

Method of Factfinding	Typical Contracting Situation
Telephone conversation to clarify limited points about the contractor's proposal.	Relatively simple requirement and low dollar value.
Face-to-face meetings consisting of either a single representative from each side or many team members from both sides, including technical specialists.	Moderate to relatively complex requirements and moderate to high dollar value.
Written request for proposal clarification, or identification of a proposal deficiency.	Relatively complex requirement where documentation is required.

With contracts of moderate to high degrees of complexity, formal face-to-face factfinding sessions and site visits with the contractor are often desirable. Since these sessions are not part of the formal negotiation phase, the contract specialist's objective is to obtain a thorough understanding of the proposal.

On less complicated proposals, factfinding may consist only of a government letter addressed to the contractor asking questions to clarify points made in the proposal. Phone calls may also be appropriate to clarify simple questions.

2.3   Assemble and Prepare Participants for Factfinding Meetings

Prepare Team   The individuals on the factfinding team are not necessarily the same people who serve on the negotiation team. Only those individuals who are designated either to ask and respond to questions, or to listen for information to help in preparing for negotiations need to attend the factfinding meeting. Conversely, some who attend the factfinding session might not be needed for the negotiation sessions.

Preparing the factfinding team includes the following responsibilities:

- Selecting factfinding team members.
- Assigning roles to members who can contribute to discussions, and assigning to other government participants the responsibility of listening to, documenting, and analyzing contractor responses.
- Briefing team members prior to the meeting with contractor representatives on their roles during the factfinding session.
- Developing questions to ask the contractor to provide or clarify information.

Technical Preparation   Technical preparation includes the following:

- Marking working copies of proposals for easy reference to questioned areas or facts.

- Sending factfinding questions to the designated contractor team leader prior to factfinding.

- Reviewing and rehearsing the planned questions so the team members can concentrate on hearing and verifying answers. It is important to prepare factfinding questions in a non-threatening form, such as:

  - How was this estimate developed?

  - What is to be provided by the proposed tasks listed on (specific) page numbers?

  - When will proposed efforts be finished?

  - Who will accomplish the proposed efforts?

  - Why are the levels of proposed efforts needed?

  - How do the proposed efforts relate to the contract specifications?

Review the proposed questions and responses beforehand to ensure that they do not unwittingly give away potential government positions or other confidential information.

Questions on Business Terms and Conditions

Since factfinding is also conducted to clarify apparent inconsistencies in the contractor proposal, questions can be used to:

- Correct clerical mistakes in the proposal.

- Obtain missing information needed to estimate price-related factors.

- Collect additional facts to clarify the proposed price or any other conditions attached to the proposed price by the contractor.

- Request additional information that may be needed to develop the price negotiation objectives. In some cases, areas of "gold-plating" can be identified for possible elimination and corresponding savings in contract price.

2.4 Conduct Factfinding

Factfinding Agenda

The three stages of effective factfinding sessions are:

- Introduction
- Detailed Interview
- Ending

<u>Introduction</u>: Introduce participants. Try to establish rapport with friendly conversation such as, "How was your trip?". Summarize the purpose and meeting agenda.

<u>Detailed Interview</u>: Maintain a professional decorum by relaxed listening and minimal interruptions. Ask questions and verify answers to finalize the government prenegotiation objectives on the proposed terms and conditions of the contract. Provide truthful and unambiguous responses to the contractor side.

<u>Ending</u>: Summarize the important things that were said by each side during the session. Clarify outstanding issues. Express appreciation to the other side. Terminate or reschedule factfinding session. Determine tentative time for bargaining session.

Dos and Don'ts of Factfinding

DO:

- Use questions as a way to begin discussions.
- Start with simple questions.
- Break complex questions into simple issues.
- Identify and rank discussion subjects and levels of concern.
- Be thorough and systematic rather than unstructured.
- Ask for the person who made the estimate to explain the amounts.
- Question the contractor until each answer is clearly understood.
- Include questions on the rationale for estimated amounts.
- Assign action items and clarification requests for incomplete answers.
- Caucus with team members to review answers and formulate the next round of questions.

DON'T:

- Negotiate price during factfinding.
- Interpret how to do a proposed effort for the contractor.
- Answer questions that other team members ask the contractor to answer.
- Allow the contractor to avoid direct answers.
- Discuss available funding or price objectives.

Length of Factfinding Session	The length of the factfinding session depends entirely on the amount and type of information needed. The factfinding session might require more time than the negotiation; this is often the case when contract specifications are not very clear, or when the proposal contains items that are not properly supported. Factfinding should continue until both sides agree on the facts. Neither side's position can be realistic until there is mutual understanding concerning the facts.
Factfinding Session	The basic communication skills during the factfinding process are: • Questioning • Probing • Listening • Understanding. Questioning: Although planning detailed questions on specific areas is desirable, non-directed and wide-ranging questions can also be advantageous. These questions are deliberately wide in scope to stimulate broad responses. This technique often produces more information in the form of unsolicited answers than a detailed questioning method. The questioning method to be chosen largely depends on the subject matter and the personality of the person to whom the questions are directed. Probing: The probing technique is useful when the contractor's answers are either vague or qualified. Probing involves a series of questions concerning the same subject matter with each successive question getting more specific to elicit a full and adequate answer. Probing also involves using different approaches or ways of asking the same question. When the answer is not satisfactory, you may ask it in another way, postpone asking the question for a while, and then rephrase the question until adequate answers are forthcoming. However, you should ensure that the questioning does not lead to an argument, which would defeat the purpose of the factfinding session. Listening: Listening is as vital to communication as talking. Inadequate communication is too often caused by inadequate listening. Moreover, the art of listening is of special significance during factfinding because the purpose of the sessions is to absorb answers by listening. Understanding: Differences in language or interpretation can often lead to misunderstandings and even unintentional disputes. To avoid this, a good technique is rephrasing a point and asking whether your interpretation is correct. Another useful technique is to share relevant portions of the technical evaluation with the contractor to show similarities and differences in the scope or statement of work.

2.5 Followup on Results of Factfinding

Revise Preliminary Negotiation Objectives

At the conclusion of the factfinding, the government factfinders will have accomplished their purpose if they have:

- Obtained a mutual understanding with the contractor on the pertinent facts pertaining to the offer,

- Tested the validity of the issues and positions identified in negotiation planning,

- Determined the assumptions and factual basis for the contractor's position, and

- Identified the contractor position on issues and the relative importance or priority the contractor places on the issues.

Amend or Cancel the RFP, if Necessary

Occasionally, factfinding reveals serious flaws in the RFP. In such a situation, consider amending the solicitation or cancelling and resoliciting the RFP.

Document

Document the results of factfinding by keeping a written record of the questions that were asked and the answers that were received during the factfinding. Generally, someone on the factfinding team should be designated as a recorder to keep a written record of what transpired during the factfinding session.

2.6 Chapter Summary

Summary

Factfinding is an important part of government contract negotiations that is needed to clarify incomplete, inconsistent, or otherwise questionable information in the contractor proposal. Although factfinding often occurs in a separate session prior to the start of actual negotiations, factfinding is a continuous process that may even be conducted at the start of the bargaining session. The government should not negotiate during factfinding since the purpose of the session is to obtain valid information on the proposal.

CHAPTER 3: NEGOTIATION PREPARATION

Learning Objectives

At the end of this chapter you will be able to:

Primary Learning Objective (PLO)
Develop a negotiation plan based on an assessment of the government's priorities and the strengths and weaknesses of all parties involved in the negotiations.

Classroom Learning Objective 3/1
Organize and brief the negotiation team.

Classroom Learning Objective 3/2
Identify the negotiation issues and objectives.

Classroom Learning Objective 3/3
Identify steps required to research the contractor's negotiation history and probable approach.

Classroom Learning Objective 3/4
Assess bargaining strengths and weaknesses of both parties.

Classroom Learning Objective 3/5
Establish negotiation priorities and potential tradeoffs or concessions.

Classroom Learning Objective 3/6
Develop a tactical plan for the negotiation.

Classroom Learning Objective 3/7
Develop the negotiation plan.

Contents and Procedures

Procedural Steps

The following flow chart outlines the steps in negotiation preparation:

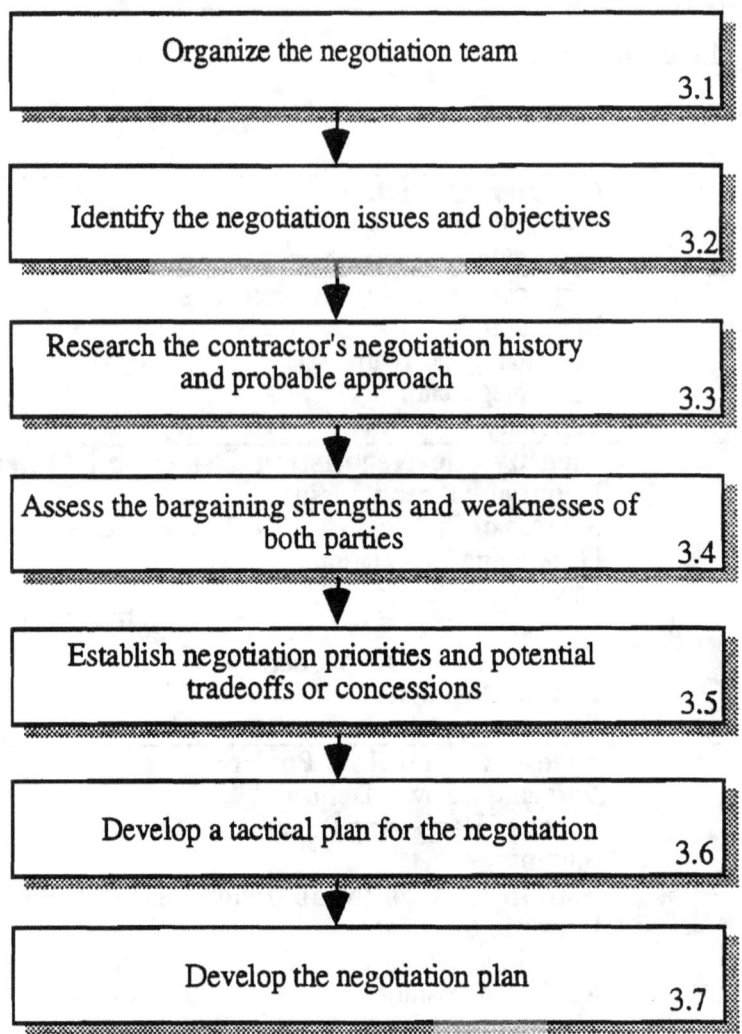

Organize the negotiation team — 3.1

Identify the negotiation issues and objectives — 3.2

Research the contractor's negotiation history and probable approach — 3.3

Assess the bargaining strengths and weaknesses of both parties — 3.4

Establish negotiation priorities and potential tradeoffs or concessions — 3.5

Develop a tactical plan for the negotiation — 3.6

Develop the negotiation plan — 3.7

3.0 Chapter Overview

Assumptions

This chapter is focused on a sole source environment. Chapter 8 will explain the differences in preparing for negotiations in a competitive environment.

The presentation in this chapter assumes that you have completed your analysis of the proposal (including any factfinding prior to the negotiation session). At this point, the government team should have in hand:

- The solicitation.
- The proposal and all data submitted by the contractor to support the proposal.
- Data from your research of the deliverable, the market for the deliverable. any relevant acquisition histories.
- Field pricing reports or audits.
- Your analysis of the proposed price and, where appropriate, of cost elements.
- Technical reviews.

Without quality data from these sources, you can neither completely prepare for nor conduct the negotiation. For the purpose of this chapter, assume that you have obtained the necessary data and are now ready to transform the data into a negotiation plan.

Importance of Preparation

The most important prerequisite to effective negotiation is thorough preparation. Neither experience, bargaining skill, nor persuasion on the part of the negotiator can compensate for the absence of preparation. Thoroughness is even more important to the government side because contractors are generally better prepared. After all, to complete the proposal, the contractor had to develop the assumptions underlying cost estimates. The contractor side is also intimately knowledgeable about a product (or service) they are providing. To minimize the inherent contractor advantage in this area, the government negotiation team must be well prepared.

Thoroughness in preparation produces tangible rewards. The quality of the contract work statement and technical descriptions will generally be improved. Pay-offs from good preparation also include:

- Fewer contract modifications because the technical requirements were well conceived during the initial negotiations; and
- Actual costs that are generally closer to estimated costs.

In short, thorough preparation improves the quality of both the contract and the contract performance.

3.1 Organize the Negotiation Team

Introduction
The first step in negotiation preparation is to determine who will represent the government at the negotiation conference. In many cases, the contract specialist is the only representative of the government side. But when a great deal of money is involved or the negotiation involves a technologically complex project, a team of specialists participates on behalf of the government.

Organizing the Team
Negotiation preparation begins with determining the size and composition of the negotiation team. The team composition depends on the size and complexity of the requirement, the circumstances surrounding the upcoming negotiation, and the personnel available to serve on the government side. Negotiation teams often consist of the contracting officer, price analyst, and technical representative. Larger teams may include auditors, engineers, legal advisors, price analysts for different cost elements, manufacturing specialists, and representatives from the program office and user community. But, some negotiation team members may not be needed at every negotiation session.

The next step is deciding on who will represent the government. Since the negotiation team is not a formal entity consisting of members from the same organization, team members are often selected from different activities. Consequently, members can be chosen from among those available individuals who are the best qualified to represent their area of expertise.

Chief Negotiator
The key person on the negotiation team is the chief or principal negotiator who does most of the bargaining and provides leadership at the negotiation session. The government team member who has the most ability as a negotiator and/or who is most knowledgeable on the procurement generally serves as the chief negotiator.

Usually the contracting officer (CO) or specialist (1102 job series) serves as the principal negotiator. Although the CO may be the only team member with the formal authority to obligate the government to contractual agreements, the CO need not be the chief negotiator. For example, a pricing specialist may serve as the principal negotiator when that team member is the most informed and capable negotiator. To take advantage of varying kinds of expertise, more than one chief negotiator can be used to bargain different issues.

Because of the importance of unity during the bargaining session, the chief negotiator should be the only individual designated to speak for the government side. However, when the chief negotiator does not have the expertise needed to respond to a particular issue, he or she can allow another team member to address the other side. Exercising this authority, the chief negotiator serves as a chairperson by "giving the floor" to another speaker. Unless this permission is granted, the other members of the government team should not speak up or address the other side during the bargaining session.

Summary

As government contracts become more complex, the team approach and role of the chief negotiator become ever more important aspects of negotiation success. The principal negotiator must bargain for the team to attain well planned objectives.

3.2 Identify the Negotiation Issues and Objectives

Identifying Potential Issues

An issue is any potential area of disagreement or an assertion about which the two sides differ. In contrast, facts are data about which both parties are likely to agree. Since the differences between facts and issues are not always clear cut, the first step in preparing for negotiations is to identify:

- Potential issues that may merit discussion. Only issues that have a material impact on either price or contract performance should be discussed.
- The government position on those issues.

A fact becomes an issue if it is challenged. Moreover, there are times when so-called "factual" information ought to become an issue but do not because the information is not challenged. Information about which negotiators agree is treated as fact and does not merit further discussion. Likewise, resolved issues become facts.

Issues are the topics of discussion in a bargaining session. Issues arise when the same subject is viewed by people with different positions and interests. Since the way issues are handled is often the key to successful negotiations, the importance of identifying and preparing for issues is paramount. Said in another way, "What can negotiators expect to clash about?" and "How can they best prepare for the ensuing discussions?"

Sources of Potential Issues and Objectives

The sources of potential issues include:

- Contractor proposals
- Factfinding notes or minutes
- Technical analysis
- Field pricing and audit reports
- The cost or price analysis
- Other proposed business terms and evaluations

Developing Negotiation Objectives

The basic goal of any negotiation is a contract that commits the contractor to providing a deliverable that:

- Will satisfy the government need (in terms of such dimensions as quality and timeliness)
- Fairly apportions risk between the government and the contractor
- Is at a fair and reasonable price
- Satisfies statutory goals, such as small business set-asides, affirmative action.

Developing the Price Objective

In contract negotiations, the focal point for the government is generally the price of the contract. The price objective is a negotiation position which should express a fair and reasonable price for the entire "package" under consideration.

Without a definite price objective, negotiations will often flounder and result in settlements that can be neither explained nor defended. Objectives such as "the lowest price we can get" or "a price about ten percent below the proposal" do not qualify as acceptable objectives because they are not in the win/win spirit and are too indefinite. Price objectives should be planned in terms of a definite dollar amount reflecting a reasonable evaluation of the terms and conditions of the intended contract.

Since the price objective represents your best judgement of a fair and reasonable price based on facts available prior to the negotiation, do not rigidly stick with that number during the course of the negotiation. Price objective is only a guide. Your judgement of what is "fair and reasonable" may change during the negotiation session as new facts become available or because of changes in your interpretation of existing data. Remember, your goal in negotiating price is not to achieve a predetermined target but rather to reach agreement on a fair and reasonable price.

When data on individual elements of cost are available, base your target position at least in part on those data. Although there may be additional costs depending on the product or service, the usual cost elements are direct material, direct labor, overhead, and general and administrative expenses. Each cost element should be estimated separately to develop a target point. In each case, the cost objective is then the point where the chances are considered equal of either exceeding or underrunning the estimate. After the objectives are set for each cost element, the sum of the elements is the total cost objective. The government price objective is then obtained when a profit factor is added to the overall cost objective.

Reasonableness of the cost estimates should be judged on the basis of the probability that such costs will occur. The price objective should be the most likely expectation of costs. Overly optimistic or pessimistic extremes should be avoided. Simply put, the price objective should be the most fair and reasonable position.

Finally, double check the price objective against available data on competitive, historical and commercial prices for the same or comparable deliverables. This reality check sometimes deflates price objectives that seemed reasonable on a cost element by cost element basis.

When negotiating without benefit of any data on elements of cost, price analysis becomes all important in determining the price objective. In this case, the target price is your best projection of the fair market value of the deliverable at the time of delivery or performance given data on competitive prices, commercial prices, historical prices and/or pricing yardsticks. You must adjust these data to account for any differences in quantities acquired, product characteristics, contractual terms and conditions, the value of the dollar at the time of award, and so forth. You must consider the relative credibility and validity of each potential price comparison. In other words, even when the price objective comes from price analysis alone, the price objective is still a matter of judgment – being your best estimate of what the government should pay for the deliverable under the circumstances.

3.3 Research the Contractor's Negotiation History and Probable Approach

How to Research

In this regard, potential sources of information may include:

- The contract proposal and all data submitted with the proposal

- Audit reports

- Previous proposals or contracts on the same kind of work

- Price Negotiation Memoranda (PNMs) with the same contractor or with other contractors for similar work

- Contract administrators, negotiators, and other government employees who have had previous dealings with the contractor

- Factfinding sessions

- Other pertinent documents from contract files of other contracts with the contractor

What to Research

Goals and Priorities: It is important to attempt to identify contractor goals and corresponding priorities. Include in your research both stated and readily apparent goals along with the unstated needs of the contractor side. While contract price is always important, every negotiation contains non-price needs and unstated needs for both sides.

Unstated Needs may include such contractor priorities as increasing market share, cash flow difficulties, or just the relative security of doing business with the government. Negotiation preparation should include consideration of such unstated needs. Government concessions that satisfy these needs often cost little or nothing, yet the government side can strongly influence the outcome of a negotiation by addressing them. (Satisfying non-price issues is covered under Rule Four, "Satisfy the Other Side's Non-Price Needs," in Chapter 5.)

Probable Styles and Tactics: An examination of the contractor's past negotiation styles, such as win/win or win/lose, and past negotiation tactics often indicates valuable information about the type of negotiators the government will face. Plan the government approach by analyzing how the contractor has negotiated in the past. For example, if the contractor side has been threatening in the past, prepare countermeasures that anticipate the use of win/lose tactics.

When you do not have experience with certain negotiators, check with your colleagues and even other federal agencies to find out about their negotiation style. The negotiation approach best suited to the situation can be selected based on the contractor's past record. Always be prepared to counter the strongest styles and to benefit from the weak negotiation styles.

Realize that assumptions as to possible future negotiation styles are just that -- assumptions. Skilled negotiators often change their approach depending on the situation. Consequently, plan your approach on the likely style of the other party, but stay flexible and be prepared to change.

Pressures and Constraints: The identification of bargaining pressures facing both sides is always an important area of research. Learning the constraints facing the government side is generally easier than identifying the pressures facing the other side. But, discovering the other side's limitations can be used to enhance your bargaining position to seek win/win outcomes. (This research is also important in applying Rule Six, "Put the Pressure on the Other Side," which will be discussed in Chapter 5.)

3.4 Assess Bargaining Power

Bargaining Power Defined

Bargaining power is never only one-sided. No one side ever has ultimate power, just as neither side is ever totally powerless.

In any negotiation, both parties have something to offer the other side or else the negotiation would not be taking place. Successful negotiators are able to recognize the actual bargaining power on each side to maximize their own strengths while minimizing the bargaining power on the other side.

Bargaining power comes in many forms. A world-renowned scientist may have bargaining power based on expertise and reputation. Suppliers often enjoy bargaining power because the government side lacks knowledge about the existence of potential competitors or substitute products. In any case, bargaining power has to be perceived by the other side to have an effect in the negotiations. When the other side does not perceive your power, your side has no edge in that regard.

Types of Bargaining Power

The following are some of the types of bargaining power to consider in assessing strengths and weaknesses of each side.

Competition: The availability or lack of competition may give one side the upper hand. Competition power is in favor of the buyer when multiple sources or alternatives are available. Conversely, sellers enjoy more competition power when availability or alternatives are limited.

However, bargaining alternatives exist even during sole source negotiations. The government side can always gain bargaining strength by researching the practicality of other alternatives, such as:

- In-house performance
- Changing requirements
- Providing start-up funds to other contractors
- Postponing contract award
- Breaking out and separately competing components

Knowledge: Which side appears to be the expert? Information is power. The more information that is known about the other side, circumstances, and the negotiation issues, the greater the bargaining power in this area. Thorough preparation can increase bargaining power based on knowledge.

Time Constraints: Which side appears to be able to use time to its advantage, e.g., time available for negotiations, time available for completion of work, date when work must start, and the expiration of funding? The advantage from this power source is apparent when time appears to work for or against the other side. Patience may strengthen this power source when the other side tries to use a deadline. (Chapter 5, Rule Seven, "Use the Power of Patience," discusses how patience can be used as a bargaining technique.)

Bargaining Skills: The use of negotiation skills gives both the perception and the reality of bargaining power. The application of the skills learned in this course should give the government side greater power in this regard because student negotiators should become better bargainers and gain more confidence in their ability to negotiate. Conversely, the contractor negotiators often lose confidence as they perceive power in the government bargaining skills.

Importance of the Contract to Each Party: As the following table shows, successful negotiation can reward both the organization and the individual. The importance of the government contract to each side is determined by how much the rewards benefit the organization and the individual participants. The side receiving the greater rewards generally tends to strive harder for success.

Organizational Rewards	Individual Rewards
Money/Profit	Increased Self-Worth
Unique Product or Service	Safety
Property	Prestige
Data Rights	Self-Esteem
Privileges	Self-Actualization
Commercial Opportunities	Security
Future Business	Reputation
Product Control	Increased Pay

Relative importance of the contract is based both on the facts and on the perceptions of each side. For example, if the contractor perceives that the contract is more important to the government than to the contractor, the contractor may be more intractable and less willing to make concessions.

Risks Inherent in the Contract: Since nothing in life is entirely risk-free, risks are inherent in every negotiated settlement. Consequently, both sides must be willing to accept varying degrees of risk.

While the risk of cost overruns or underruns can be shifted to either the contractor or the government depending on the type of contract, cost risk can never be completely avoided. Even a fixed price contract contains some cost risk for the government because the government "risks" paying for a product or service that may not meet performance expectations or may no longer be necessary.

Most negotiated agreements are based on estimates of what future costs will be. However, actual costs are rarely the same as what is estimated. Even the best estimates are either too high or too low, but never precisely equal to actual costs. Consequently, while seeking lower degrees of risk for their side, negotiators must still be prepared to accept some degree of risk.

The side most willing to take risks gains more bargaining power in this area. Since security and risk avoidance are natural tendencies, the negotiator willing to accept greater degrees of risk or uncertainty increases bargaining power.

Summary

Bargaining power comes in many forms and is never totally one-sided. The recognition of different types of bargaining power in a negotiation helps government negotiators better understand the bargaining strengths and weaknesses of both sides.

3.5 Establish Negotiation Priorities and Positions

Prioritize the Issues

Rank the many potential issues in order of importance to the government. After ranking, determine whether each issue is:

- Essentially nonnegotiable ("must points")
- Open to trade or concession ("give points")
- Something to avoid discussing ("avoid points")
- Open to bargaining ("bargaining points")

"Must points" are those issues that normally cannot be conceded because of their importance to the government side. Conversely, "give points" can be used as concessions because they are issues that are relatively low in importance to the government side but may be valuable to the contractor. "Avoided points" are those issues that, because of some element of weakness or inflexibility, the government does not want to discuss. "Bargaining points" are issues that will generally be subject to offers and counteroffers that fall somewhere between the opening positions of the two sides. For instance, price is a bargaining point, in that the government and contractor typically reach agreement on a dollar value between their opening bargaining positions.

Determine the Price Range

Negotiators need to have more than one price position available when negotiating fixed-price contracts. Different positions are necessary to give the government negotiators bargaining room and identify the maximum reasonable price or price ceiling. In addition, negotiations on the other than firm fixed price contracts require bargaining on other price related targets. For example, the share ratios and ceiling price are negotiated on fixed price incentive firm contracts. Likewise, minimum and maximum fees in cost plus incentive fee contracts are determined through negotiations. The government minimum and maximum positions on these price related issues should be identified during preparation.

Minimum Position

The minimum price position is the first government counter-offer. In a win/win negotiation, the minimum price should be equivalent to the lowest fair and reasonable price. The minimum price may also indicate the amount of concessions necessary to reach the price objective or target.

The use of arbitrary "nice low figures" as a minimum position is neither defensible nor appropriate. The opening price position should be calculated with the same fair logic used in determining win/win price objectives. Using arbitrarily low minimum positions is not in the win/win spirit and may even be counterproductive. An indefensible or unreasonable opening position often causes the government to lose credibility. Even when the government side plans for win/win settlements, loss of credibility caused by unreasonable openings makes attaining win/win outcomes more difficult.

The minimum price should be determined on the reasonable probability of incurring the costs given a best case scenario. However, negotiators will still have to accept the slight risk that under the most favorable circumstances, actual contract costs may be lower than the minimum position. Nevertheless, win/win minimums should be developed under "reasonable" favorable assumptions and not unlikely "pie in the sky" scenarios.

Government negotiators should determine a minimum position for each major element of contract cost and profit. Besides serving as the lowest estimate of reasonable cost, minimum positions give the government side bargaining space. Concessions can then be made during the negotiation because the minimum is, in effect, just the government's opening position. (The importance of bargaining room is discussed later in Chapter 5 under Rule Two, "Give Yourself Room to Compromise.")

Maximum Position

Since price objectives are sometimes exceeded, a maximum position should also be developed. Like the process for determining the minimum position, the maximum position is estimated on the basis of the probability of incurring the cost. In contrast to the minimum position, the maximum is determined on the reasonable probability of least favorable circumstances or highest costs. Using the *reasonable* "worst case" scenario facts and assumptions, the government side determines maximum price by estimating the highest contract price for such a scenario. However, highly unlikely assumptions should be disregarded in making this determination.

The maximum position could instead be the amount of available funds or ceiling price when the authority of the negotiator or the available funding is between the price objective and the "true maximum" estimated using the methodology in the preceding paragraph. This maximum position is defensible even though the amount is less than the highest price that could be considered fair and reasonable.

Non-price Needs

Many other bargaining issues besides price are always present in every negotiation, such as:

- Contract type
- Warranties
- Delivery schedule
- Other business terms and conditions

Compare Government and Contractor Positions

For meaningful evaluation to occur, the positions of the two sides must be compared. As illustrated in the following diagram, such a comparison readily shows the reasons for the different positions.

Issues: Direct Labor Production Hours

Government Position: 500 Hours ⟷	Contractor Position: 700 Hours
Supporting Evidence:	Supporting Evidence:
• 68% learning curve indicated ⟷ • Greater experience in labor mix than previously	• 75% learning curve slope used • Assumption that labor mix experience will remain the same

3.6 Develop a Negotiation Approach

Determine the Order in which Issues will be Discussed

The order of mention of issues should be planned carefully. Some plans start with the least important issues and proceed to the more important ones. Under this approach, concessions can be made on less important issues with the hope that fewer concessions will be needed on the more important issues. Other plans arrange issues according to the anticipated ease of reaching agreement. This way there is greater likelihood of reaching agreement early and creating an atmosphere of agreement that will, it is hoped, continue to the harder issues.

Rehearse Potential Concessions

Concession making is vital to reaching negotiated agreement. Accordingly, the government side should rehearse potential trades by planning on what concessions the contractor side is expected to make in order to "win" a government concession. (In Chapter 5 under the discussion of bargaining techniques, we will discuss concession making in detail under Rule Two, "Give Yourself Room To Compromise," and Rule Five, "Use Concessions Wisely.")

Contract price reductions in a sole source negotiating environment can be accomplished by using such tradeoffs as changing contract type, providing government financing, and increasing optional purchases. Changing contract type from fixed price to one of the cost-reimbursable varieties can reduce contract price by reducing contractor cost risk. Similarly, government financing arrangements, such as progress payments or earlier acceptance, often lowers price by enhancing contractor cash flow. Offering option purchases can also reduce contract cost by increasing economies of scale.

Plan Bargaining Tactics

The selection of negotiation tactics largely depends on the research as to the probable tactics expected of the contractor side. **However, since an important concern of the government is always attainment of a win/win outcome, limit or entirely avoid the application of win/lose tactics.** (Chapter 6 will discuss the most commonly used negotiation tactics.)

The successful application of negotiation tactics requires a great deal of planning. The negotiator must be prepared to respond in a manner that protects the government and makes progress toward agreement. This preparation is accomplished by anticipating the probable contractor tactics and developing countermeasures in advance.

3.7 Develop the Negotiation Plan

Prepare a Negotiation Plan

Draft a negotiation plan that includes the following information:

- Background (contract, contractor, negotiating situation)
- Major and minor issues (including non-price needs)
- Target positions (include price objective, opening and maximum positions)
- Tactical plan
- Team members and roles

Brief Management on the Plan

Before the start of negotiations, the negotiating team briefs government officials to review the upcoming negotiation. This meeting gives government management the opportunity to provide input on the negotiation as well as give policy guidance and support in the handling of particular problems or issues. This briefing generally occurs between factfinding and the actual negotiation.

The prenegotiation briefings can take many forms. This review can be a five-minute rundown of the facts and objectives when the upcoming negotiation is a small or routine contract. The meeting can also take the form of a formal flip chart presentation or slide show for the agency's top procurement managers. Or, the briefing may not take the form of a meeting if management is provided written justification or a business clearance for permission to proceed as intended with the upcoming negotiation.

Whatever the form of the prenegotiation briefing, obtaining management concurrence is extremely important. The government bargainers must know they have management support and the authority to maintain or deviate from the price objective. Moreover, management should identify any priorities or limitations during the prenegotiation conference. Consultation with management may also be an on-going requirement during negotiation, particularly when unanticipated problems develop or when new alternatives need to be considered.

Prepare Negotiation Agenda

One of the most difficult tasks during a negotiation is to confine the discussion to what is important while avoiding irrelevant subjects. One of the best ways to promote productive and efficient discussion is to establish an agenda for both sides to follow.

Agendas are usually presented at the start of the bargaining session by the government's chief negotiator. When applicable, copies of the agenda could be provided to the contractor side before negotiations start. Even consider obtaining contractor input to the agenda as a courtesy and a means to encourage cooperation.

The negotiation agenda should include the following items:

- Topics to be discussed and order of mention.
- Proposed time schedule for the negotiation sessions.
- Location(s) of the negotiation session(s).
- Names and titles of government and contractor team members. Include office symbols and phone numbers when appropriate.

Rehearse and Finalize the Negotiation Plan	Things to consider in finalizing and rehearsing the negotiation plan include: • Presenting the plan to the team members. • Obtaining agreement on the role each member will play. • Conducting a simulated negotiation session, including role playing. • Using "devil's advocates" to challenge the government position with arguments favoring the contractor position. Rehearse government responses and counters to the "devil's advocate" challenges.
Conduct Initial Briefing Of Team Members (Kickoff Briefing)	Before the negotiations begin, the chief negotiator should brief team members on the correct procedures to be adhered to during the bargaining session. Particular emphasis should be on the chief negotiator's role as principal speaker and "chairperson" of the government side. The team is usually composed of individuals from different organizations who may never have participated in a government contract negotiation. In addition, some team members may be accustomed to leadership roles in their regular jobs and may find it difficult not to speak out during the negotiations. Team members need to fully understand their function and what they can and cannot do during negotiations. **They must realize that the chief negotiator is the government's spokesperson and the only individual who is authorized to negotiate with the contractor.** In contrast, the functions of the team members are to provide support, listen, evaluate, and handle any specific issues that the chief negotiator may assign to them. Since team members may address the contractor side only when so instructed by the chief negotiator, they should not give direct replies even if asked a direct question by a contractor representative. In this case, team members should seek approval from the principal negotiator before responding. A polite way to obtain approval for a response would be to ask the chief negotiator, "Would you rather answer that one, or shall I?" Responding to direct questions can also be delegated by the use of prearranged signals between the chief negotiator and the team members. Key points for the initial or "kickoff" briefing include: • Restatement of government overall goals: Negotiate a fair and reasonable price in a win/win atmosphere resulting in quality products and timely performance • Roles and responsibilities of each team member • A reminder not to address the contractor side unless directed by the chief negotiator • Prohibition of ex parte communications with the contractor side (outside the negotiation conference)

- A warning to safeguard confidential information from the contractor or other unauthorized persons
- Ethical considerations, such as no free lunches or favored treatment
- Emphasis that the primary contract price objective is the total contract price, and not necessarily the cost of individual cost elements

---

3.8 Summary

Summary   Successful negotiation outcomes often depend on the thoroughness of preparations made beforehand. During this period, it is necessary to decide who will be on the negotiation team and who will be the chief negotiator. Preparation time is needed to establish the negotiating objectives and specific issues, and to evaluate the probable negotiation style and approaches of the other side. Additionally, time is needed to identify potential concessions and to assess the bargaining power of each side. Building on this information, the government team should prepare an overall approach and plan for obtaining the negotiation objectives. Finally, the government team needs time to rehearse and finalize the negotiation plan.

CHAPTER 4: CONDUCTING NEGOTIATIONS

Learning Objectives

At the end of this chapter you will be able to:

Primary Learning Objective (PLO)
Conduct government contract negotiations.

Classroom Learning Objective 4/1
Prepare the negotiation environment.

Classroom Learning Objective 4/2
Negotiate.

Classroom Learning Objective 4/3
Prepare the Price Negotiation Memorandum (PNM).

Contents and Procedures

Procedural Steps

The following flowchart outlines the information presented in this chapter:

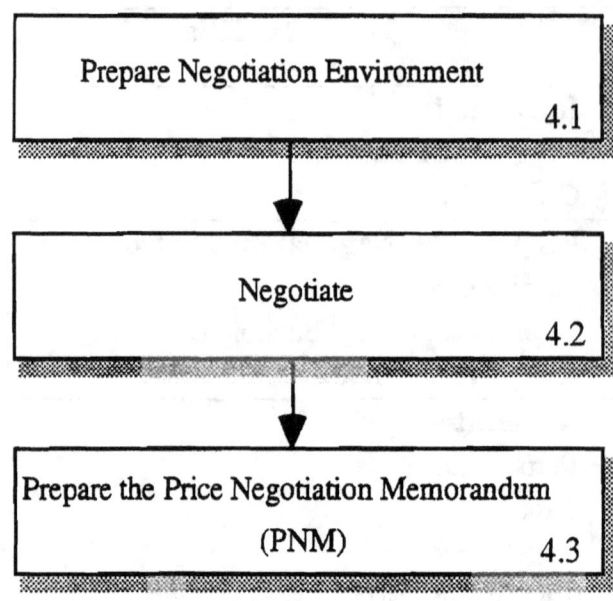

4.0 Introduction

Negotiation Phase

The negotiation stage of the government contract process is the phase in which the actual bargaining with the contractor is conducted. The length of the negotiation varies for each contract, from a single conference to many bargaining sessions stretching over days and even weeks. The time needed to negotiate depends on the complexity of contract, number of issues, and differences between the two parties, as well as the personalities and styles of the individual negotiators.

Chapter Context

The negotiations discussed in this chapter include only sole source contracts. Much of the material is also applicable to competitive discussions, which are not included here, but are covered in Chapter 8.

4.1 Prepare the Negotiation Environment

Introduction

Achieving win/win outcomes should be the paramount priority for most government contract negotiations and the negotiation environment can aid the attainment of these desired outcomes. The physical and psychological atmosphere surrounding the bargaining session can have an important impact on the type of outcome perceived by each side.

Prepare the Physical Environment

The government usually hosts the bargaining session. When it does, it then has the responsibility for providing the facilities in which a negotiation can be conducted. In preparing the facilities, remember that the physical arrangements should facilitate win/win outcomes and that your side is "selling" a position. Consequently, the physical environment should enhance these overriding themes by giving the other side the perception they are being treated fairly and with respect. Although the physical environment also conveys many important nonverbal messages which will be discussed in Chapter 7, some important things to consider are:

- Conduct the negotiation in a room with sufficient comfort for both sides, to include adequate furnishings, lighting, and space for each side. Ensuring a comfortable room temperature is also important. Physical discomfort may negatively affect the attitudes of people already under negotiating pressure who often perceive discomfort as a win/lose tactic by the host side.

- Conference table(s) large enough to comfortably seat all members of both teams with adequate space for their work papers, reference material, and briefcases should be provided. Depending upon the complexity of and probable length of the negotiation, more chairs may be needed if specialists or observers are added to the group. However, any additional furniture should be positioned so as not to interfere with the action at the negotiation table.

- Try to arrange for nearby caucus rooms that could be available for confidential conferences to allow each side privacy during recesses for solving problems and re-examining positions.

- Provide necessary visual aids support for both negotiating teams. This may include overhead projectors, VCR/TV, and display charts. White boards and chalkboards are especially useful during price negotiations. Good visual aids for presenting facts and historical data that both sides agree on is generally beneficial to negotiations.

Rebrief Team Members

Brief team members immediately prior to negotiations on their individual roles during the bargaining session and review the important points of the kickoff briefing (see Chapter 3).

Be prompt. The government team members should arrive on time --in fact, preferably before the team members from the other side.

Since successful negotiations are founded on mutual respect between the parties, personal appearance is important. The team leader, along with each team member should ensure that everyone on the government team presents a neat and well-groomed appearance. The importance of personal appearance will be discussed in greater detail in Chapter 7.

4.2 Negotiate

Introduction

Conducting negotiations can be broken down into 7 tasks:

(1) Opening
(2) Factfinding
(3) Discussing Issues
(4) Reaching Agreements
(5) Managing the Team
(6) Taking Breaks/Caucus
(7) Closing

Task 1: Opening

The opening of the conference is critical because it sets the stage for the rest of the negotiations. The manner of the opening can influence attitudes that will prevail throughout the conference and can either aid or detract from a win/win agreement.

The government team leader is responsible for opening the conference with a statement and presenting the agenda. The opening statement generally consists of background information to facilitate mutual understanding. Since the conference opening should be planned beforehand, the following suggestions should be considered.

- Extend a firm handshake and cordial greeting to everyone while expressing appreciation for the contractor's interest in obtaining the government contract (see Chapter 7).

- Introduce government team members by their full names, titles or positions. To help both sides remember each others' names, consider providing an attendance roster or nameplates for all team members at the conference table. If the nameplates have been prepositioned on the table, allow time for the contractor side to rearrange the seating in accordance with their seating preference.

- Strive to dispel the tension present at every negotiation. Casual conversation often reduces tension and helps conferees feel at ease. But most importantly, emphasize the government's interest in fairness and a win/win outcome. Ask the other side to maintain an objective attitude and solicit their sincere cooperation.

Task 2: Factfinding

After the opening remarks, the chief negotiator should not delve immediately into the major issues of the negotiation. Instead, the first order of business should generally be to ensure that both parties have the same understanding of:

- The work to be done
- Government terms and conditions for performing the work
- Exceptions to those terms and conditions proposed by the contractor
- Facts, assumptions, and judgments submitted by the contractor to support its proposal

If factfinding preceded the formal negotiation conference, summarize the results of the session. Then allow time for any further factfinding that either party may feel is necessary. Also remember that factfinding does not necessarily end once the actual bargaining begins. Continued factfinding is often necessary because both parties often dispute the assumptions and judgments of the other side.

If factfinding has been scheduled or if there has been no factfinding at all prior to this point proceed with the factfinding session — observing the rules for factfinding discussed in Chapter 2.

Task 3: Discussing Issues

The government should maintain the initiative throughout the discussions by controlling the agenda, asking the questions, and holding to the negotiation plan. However, the government side also needs to be flexible by adjusting to the negotiation methods of the contractor side. For example, the government side may need to employ tactics or countermeasures to achieve the desired win/win outcome when the tactics displayed by the contractor side demonstrate a win/lose negotiating style.

Remember to actively listen to what the other side is saying. Since you have two ears and one mouth, listen to what is being said twice as often as you talk. Listening will minimize the probability of misunderstanding and also show you have a genuine interest in what the other side is saying.

Contract Requirements

Discussions generally begin with both parties seeking agreement on the contract requirements and the related aspects of the Contract Schedule (Sections A through H of the Uniform Contract Format). Until there is a meeting of the minds on all contract characteristics, negotiations on contract price cannot proceed.

When discussing technical issues, always be mindful of the potential impact on price. Remember that every contract requirement, such as the specifications or delivery schedule, can dramatically increase contract costs. For this reason, do not get boxed into a high price by prematurely agreeing with recommendations for "gold plating" the deliverable.

Nevertheless, there may be reasons for revisiting the schedule after agreement has been reached and price negotiations have started. Earlier agreements are always negotiable until a final settlement on contract price has been reached. For instance, the agreed upon delivery schedule could be changed by mutual agreement if the contractor would agree on a lower price in exchange for a different delivery schedule.

Contract Price

The basic way for the government to negotiate price depends on whether the contractor offer is below or above the lowest government estimate of a fair and reasonable price consistent with a win/win outcome. (NOTE: For certain contract types, other contract price issues are also negotiated. For example, when negotiating fixed price incentive firm contracts, agreement must be obtained on the ceiling price and share ratios.)

Negotiating Low Offers

When the contractor has proposed a price that is significantly below the minimum government position on what constitutes a fair and reasonable price, the government should treat the offer as a potential "mistake" under FAR 15.607. The thrust of the negotiations then may be to determine whether or not the contractor can be considered responsive at that price. FAR 9.103(c) stresses that "the award of a contract to a supplier based on lowest evaluated price alone can be false economy if there is subsequent default, late deliveries, or other unsatisfactory performance resulting in additional contractual or administrative costs."

FAR 15.608 also stresses that the purpose of price or cost analysis is "not only to determine whether [the offered price] is reasonable, but also to determine the contractor's understanding of the work and ability to perform the contract." When negotiating a low offer, these issues may become paramount. Sometimes, the contractor side will discover that there is more to the work than they had anticipated, in which case a higher priced offer may be submitted. If the contractor successfully demonstrates that the work can and will be satisfactorily performed at the offered price, then you may award at that price even if the contractor knows that a profit will probably not be achievable at that price.

Negotiating High Offers

In sole source negotiations, the proposed price is usually significantly higher than the government minimum. How the government negotiates with the contractor to lower that price depends on whether certified data on contractor costs is available. Since the contractor may have valid reasons to demonstrate that its initial proposed price is more reasonable than the government position, in a true win/win spirit never completely rule out that possibility and insist on a price reduction.

If the contractor has submitted cost data, the negotiations should generally be conducted in the following order:

* The proposed work design (i.e., the work breakdown structure).
* Direct costs (i.e., materials, labor, and other) of performing the work.
* Indirect costs, such as overhead and general and administrative costs.
* Profit or fee.
* The overall contract price.

Do not become preoccupied with any single element of cost by insisting on reaching agreement on every cost element. The government goal should be to achieve a mutual agreement on an overall price that is fair and reasonable.

When negotiating on the basis of price analysis alone (with no accompanying cost analysis), use the following method of persuasion to reach agreement on a lower price. First, present the reasons for believing that the offered price is too high, such as historical prices, other commercial prices or the government estimate. Next, place the burden on the contractor to prove that the offered price is reasonable and fair to both parties, e.g., by volunteering limited or partial cost data.

Task 4: Reaching Agreements	Begin by identifying and laying aside those issues on which the government agrees with the contractor position. Next, attempt to resolve the remaining issues to your mutual benefit. When differences cannot be resolved, pursue agreement through the give and take of bargaining by trading "gains" for "losses."
Sequencing Areas of Disagreement	There are different schools of thought on the best sequence for negotiating areas of disagreement. One school believes it is better to start by negotiating those issues that are of greatest importance and then discuss the less important issues. As each issue comes up, try to reach agreement. When agreement cannot be reached, lay the issue aside and move on to the next. Once you begin discussing issues of secondary importance, you can trade these secondary issues for the more important unresolved issues.
	Another school of thought believes it is best to start negotiating on secondary issues first. Because secondary issues are often easier to agree on, this approach creates a climate of success and mutual cooperation. Advocates of this approach feel that the favorable climate makes it easier to reach agreement on the more important issues.
	Finally, a third school of thought suggests that the government negotiate the contractor demands first. According to this approach, by first making concessions on items important to the contractor, the government side creates a win/win environment and is then more likely to receive comparable concessions from the contractor side.
	No one approach is necessarily better than another. The issues being negotiated, circumstances surrounding the negotiation, and the negotiating styles of the negotiator determine the method most likely to succeed. Moreover, predictable patterns may not even be desirable when regularly negotiating with the same party.
Agreement Through Mutual Problem-Solving	The initial approach to resolving areas of disagreement is to determine if the government and contractor sides can mutually solve the problems that divide them. Mutual problem-solving involves attempts to overcome this conflict by agreeing to alternative solutions satisfactory to both parties.
	For example, although most contractors want to own the technical data generated by their contract, this condition is generally unacceptable to the government. The government side wants the data available for competitive follow-on acquisitions while the contractor does not want to give competitors access to proprietary information. The seemingly unresolvable problem can often be worked out by contractual language that protects the rights of both parties.
Agreement Through Tradeoffs	It is not always possible to resolve conflicting positions by developing solutions that satisfy both sides. Some issues will involve differences on which neither side can agree because each side feels its position can be supported with logic and fact. When this occurs, the negotiators will have to attempt to reach agreement through the process of trading. Each party will have to make a concession that is important to its side. A concession made on one issue is traded by getting the other party to concede on a different issue.

- Skill is required in knowing how and when to make concessions. (Wise concession making is covered in Chapter 5.) Some skilled negotiators believe it is preferable to get the other side to make the first concession because the side that makes the first concession is often more likely to concede the most. Other good bargainers want to make the first concession to set the tone for a win/win environment which will, in turn, facilitate concessions from the other side.

- Counteroffers should be supportable and represent a reasonable government position. However, counteroffers should generally be somewhat conservative but still appear reasonable. Large concessions leave no room for further room for maneuvering. In addition, large numbers of small concessions will more likely demonstrate fairness and reasonableness than one or two large concessions.

- Provide sufficient justification to convincingly demonstrate the merits of the government position. Also give the contractor team time alone to review the government counter. Likewise, a recess after contractor counteroffers is often beneficial to enable the government to examine the merits of the new position. When necessary, seek advice from outside experts to prepare the next government offer.

- When a midpoint between the government and contractor position is acceptable, consider splitting the difference evenly. However, the difference between the two respective positions should be very small before the "split" occurs. Moreover, further bargaining on the issues should be avoided after a "split" has occurred. Efforts to continue more "splits" resemble auctions and are detrimental to negotiator credibility.

- When there are still some remaining issues, try to reach final agreement by combining the outstanding issues. When the unresolved issues represent a small part of the total deal, this technique may quickly bring a final resolution of all remaining issues. For example, this technique can be successfully applied when material costs and the profit remain unresolved by combining the issues and attempting to reach agreement on total price.

- Keep a written record of offers, counteroffers, agreements, and unresolved issues. This list can be helpful in showing what the positions were and what each side agreed to.

Task 5: Managing the Team

The chief negotiator, as government team leader during the negotiations, must know when to call on the members of the team. The lead negotiator must continually exercise the positive control necessary to ensure effective communications while presenting a unified position to the contractor side.

The chief negotiator must also be prepared to interrupt when team members become overeager and enter into an uncontrolled discussion with the contractor. For example, the lead negotiator might say "I'm going to interrupt you because I think we're getting off the track" or "I'm a little unclear on this point myself, and I'd like to discuss this privately with my team before we continue."

Task 6: Taking Breaks/Caucus

Frequent breaks should be taken by the government side in order to control the pace of the negotiations and to ensure private team discussions. Breaks afford the negotiation team time away from the conference table to privately assess new information and re-evaluate its position. Because of the lack of privacy, team caucuses should not be attempted in the negotiation conference room. Breaking in a separate area also permits the negotiation team to consult other individuals either in person or over the telephone without the other side knowing.

Breaks are generally called when one party wants to give the other side the opportunity to evaluate a position or concession. Caucuses are also used to restore team control when one team member has spoken out of turn. Use breaks to help restore a cordial and unemotional atmosphere when emotional or provocative statements are made, or to calm down individuals who have become contentious. In addition, breaks are extremely useful in providing refreshing relief from the stress of the negotiation. Any team members could also request a recess when an important point has been missed or if the chief negotiator did not take advantage of an opening that the contractor has provided.

Caucuses may help divert the discussion from sensitive issues or areas of weakness because the discussions resumed after the break do not always begin precisely where they ended. A skilled negotiator can often steer the ensuing discussion around the sensitive issues once the discussion resumes.

Task 7: Closing

The negotiation should be closed as soon as possible once both sides reach general agreement. Do not prolong discussions any longer than necessary. Because the purpose of the bargaining session is to reach a deal, seize the moment by exhibiting your conviction that the agreement is at hand.

A wavering party that is uncertain that the deal is in its best interest may be swayed by assurances, such as, "What we have agreed to is in our mutual interests," or "I'm confident that we both have a good deal." When the other side is still reluctant, show anticipation that a deal has been reached by discussing the wording of the agreement. Focusing attention on your intent to enter into an agreement may provide the push needed for final acceptance. Discussions on the wording of the agreement could also be combined with questions about starting the project, such as "When would you like to begin work?"

Another way to close is to summarize the areas of mutual agreement and extend a handshake as a gesture of closure. In this regard, reviewing interim agreements on major portions of the contract may also be beneficial in obtaining final overall agreement.

4.3 Prepare the Price Negotiation Memorandum

The Need for Documentation

A negotiated contract pricing action must be supported by written evidence demonstrating that the price is fair and reasonable. This evidence must be in sufficient detail to record the significant considerations established in the negotiated contract price.

Reports of analyses and requests for specific information contribute to the factual basis for determining that the offered price is fair and reasonable. The Price Negotiation Memorandum (PNM), and supporting reports of analysis, are used in reviews preceding approval of the proposed contract and in future acquisitions. Because of the number of contract actions, contracting personnel turnover, or the use of contract files in historical research, this memorandum must permit a rapid reconstruction of the major considerations in pricing the contract.

Price Negotiation Memorandum (PNM)

The official contract file must include written documents demonstrating, clearly and conclusively, what was agreed to in regards to price, terms and conditions, schedule, and work requirements. The documents must show all significant facts considered in reaching agreement with the contractor.

After negotiations have been concluded, the contracting officer must document the results of the negotiation and tell the story of the negotiation using the format of the PNM prescribed for your contracting activity. The following questions that must be addressed by the PNM.

- What was the offer and what were the costs in the SF 1411?

- What was the government price objective and what were the costs supporting that goal?

- What cost or pricing data were submitted but not relied on and not used?

- What were the goals as to delivery and pricing arrangement?

- What was discussed?

- What were the compelling arguments?

- What disposition was made of the principal points raised in preliminary analyses, included in the objective, and discussed in the negotiations?

- What cost values support the agreed-to price?

- If different from those supporting the objective, what justifications are there for the differences?

The PNM is also used as a sales document to establish the reasonableness of the agreement reached with the company. This document is the permanent record of the negotiation that charts the progress from proposal through agreement. The PNM is the source document when it becomes necessary to reconstruct the events of the procurement. A written record is also needed because the members of the negotiating team may either not remember or not be available when questions are raised.

PNMs are written by the CO or a representative from the negotiating team. Depending upon the organization, this may be the price analyst or contract negotiator. In any event, it should be an individual who actively participated in negotiation of the pricing arrangement.

Among the data generated by the end of the negotiation are:

• The price proposal
• Supporting schedules
• Subcontractor cost or pricing data
• Revised and supplementary data

Additional data will be from the government personnel who provided supporting analyses. Collectively, the documentation should show what data were available.

The PNM explains the data, including:

• The identification of significant factual data
• Explanation of how the facts influenced estimates of costs
• Which factors persuaded the negotiator that a specific figure was the one to use

The PNM will also show factual data submitted and not used, and specifically identify any cost or pricing data found to be inaccurate, incomplete, or not current.

The question of length is a critical one, because it is very easy to go into great detail in reporting the events of an extended negotiation. The writer must guard against excessive detail, and perhaps just as importantly, against using jargon. The level of detail and style in the PNM is determined by the audience of the document, which generally consists of the government officials who have the final say on whether the contract is approved.

The differences in the level of PNM detail and complexity is often caused by the amount of actual cost and performance data available and relevant to the negotiation. The availability of data will shape the course of analysis and dictate the kind and amounts of information to include in the PNM. The existence of meaningful actual costs should make it possible to be quite precise in explaining what was done and why it made good sense to do it.

The PNM format as extracted from FAR .

• The purpose of the negotiation

• A description of the acquisition, including appropriate identifying numbers

- The name, position, and organization of each person representing the contractor and the government in the negotiation.

If certified cost or pricing data were required, the extent to which the contracting officer:

- Relied on the cost or pricing data submitted and used them in negotiating the price; and

- Recognized as inaccurate, incomplete, or not current any cost or pricing data submitted; the action taken by the contracting officer and the contractor as a result; and the effect of the defective data on the price negotiated.

A summary of the contractor's proposal contains the field pricing report recommendations, and the reasons for any pertinent variances from these recommendations. Where the determination of price reasonableness is based on cost analysis, the summary shall address the amount of each major cost element:

- Proposed by the contractor
- Recommended by the field or other pricing assistance report (if any)
- Contained in the government's negotiation objective
- Considered negotiated as a part of the price

The most significant facts or circumstances controlling the establishment of the prenegotiation price objective and the negotiated price including an explanation of any significant differences between the two positions. To the extent such direction is received, the PNM shall discuss and quantify the impact of direction given by Congress, other agencies, and higher level officials if the direction has had a significant impact on the action.

4.4 Summary

Summary   Careful adherence to appropriate conduct of government contract negotiations helps ensure a fair and reasonable price for the government and contractor sides. Proper negotiation conduct begins with the preparation of the negotiating environment and the personal introductions at the start of the bargaining session. During the negotiations, the government negotiator can use a variety of bargaining methods to resolve conflict and reach agreement. But throughout the bargaining session, the chief negotiator should focus on using logic and persuasion to present the government position . A win/win outcome beneficial to both sides is more important to the government than obtaining the contract at the lowest possible price. Finally, the PNM should clearly document how the price was derived by showing what facts were considered in reaching agreement with the contractor.

CHAPTER 5: BARGAINING TECHNIQUES

Learning Objectives

At the end of this chapter you will be able to:

Primary Learning Objective
Apply the bargaining techniques.

Classroom Learning Objective 5/1
Aim high.

Classroom Learning Objective 5/2
Give yourself room to compromise.

Classroom Learning Objective 5/3
Do not volunteer weaknesses.

Classroom Learning Objective 5/4
Satisfy non-price needs.

Classroom Learning Objective 5/5
Use concessions wisely.

Classroom Learning Objective 5/6
Put the pressure on the other side.

Classroom Learning Objective 5/7
Use the power of patience.

Classroom Learning Objective 5/8
Be willing to walk away from or back to negotiations.

Classroom Learning Objective 5/9
Say it right.

Classroom Learning Objective 5/10
Be prepared.

Contents and Procedures

5.0 Introduction

Techniques That Win

Successful negotiators use a variety of different negotiation skills but research has shown that most winning negotiators share many universally accepted bargaining techniques. These precepts constitute the most important rules on what to do and what not to do in order to win at negotiations. Moreover, these winning precepts universally apply to all types of contract negotiations, including those bargaining sessions where there are other issues besides contract price.

5.1 Rule 1: Aim High

Relevance for Successful Negotiators

The slogan "Aim High" has a great deal of relevance for successful negotiators because the expectation level of negotiators is closely related to the outcome of the negotiations. While the expectation level is not the opening position or the asking price, it is still the gauge by which people measure their performance. Generally, the higher the expectations, the better the negotiators will ultimately perform. The reason for this relationship is that expectations influence the behavior of the negotiators and it is that behavior which influences the outcome of the bargaining session.

Relation Between Expectations and Performance

The strong correlation between expectations and performance should come as no surprise because it affects many facets of our lives. Norman Vincent Peale focused on the importance of a good attitude in his book, *The Power of Positive Thinking*. Said in another way, you have a better chance at success if you think you will do well. Conversely, people who think they will not succeed will generally do poorly. This theme is constantly demonstrated in everyday life. The basketball coach increases the odds of winning the big game by telling his players how much better their team is compared to their opponents, instead of focusing on the team's weak areas.

Research has shown a strong relationship between expectation level and the outcome of negotiations. Under identical circumstances student sellers who expected to receive more for their product (high expectation level) generally received a higher price than sellers with lower aspirations. Similarly, student buyers who had high expectation levels tended to pay less than their counterparts who faced identical pressures but had lower expectation levels.

Unknown Pressures

When first establishing expectation levels, good negotiators often go beyond their initial expectations. The reason is that negotiators, like people in general, are naturally more aware of their own personal pressures and limitations than they are aware of the pressures facing the other side. Because of this phenomenon, buyers are often willing to pay more than necessary, while sellers often expect an outcome that is less than what they could get if they brought higher expectations to the negotiation.

The sale of automobiles in the classified used car ads is a good example of this phenomenon. Private party sellers frequently sell their cars for less money than what the vehicles are actually worth because they are **more aware** of their own personal pressures along with the actual and potential problems of the vehicle being sold. Moreover, the same private party sellers have no knowledge of the pressures facing the nameless strangers who respond to their newspaper want ads. Similarly, car buyers are acutely aware of the personal pressures associated with the car purchase, such as their urgent need for transportation, and know little or nothing of the actual pressures facing the private party seller. This ignorance of the pressure facing the other party explains why the expectation levels of otherwise good negotiators are frequently not as high as they should be.

Make Positive Assumptions

The key to establishing high expectations is developing positive assumptions about your bargaining position. Positive assumptions lead to high expectations while negative assumptions lead to low expectations.

The $18,000 blue book value of an automobile is a good illustration of this phenomena. A seller making poor assumptions will assume that $18,000 is the most he/she could get for the car. In contrast, sellers with positive assumptions will assume that the blue book price represents an "average" price which means some cars sold for more than $18,000 and some for less. Sellers making the positive assumptions will believe they will be among the sellers to sell at higher than average. Making this favorable assumption will give these sellers high expectation levels.

Caution

Government negotiators should avoid the tendency to base their expectations for a price approximating the amount of funds available for the contract. Government negotiators should not "Aim High" by lowering their price objective when available funding is less than their estimate of a fair and reasonable price. Likewise, the price objective should not be increased just because funds are available.

In government contract negotiations, high expectations should be more than just obtaining contracts at good prices. Government negotiators "Aim High" by striving for win/win outcomes and high expectations on non-price needs, such as quality. Having expectations of negotiating a contract price below what the government considers fair and reasonable is really aiming low and likely to result in win/lose or lose/lose outcomes.

5.2 Rule 2: Give Yourself Room to Compromise

Relevance

Concession making is essential to successfully conducting most negotiations. Even the most skilled bargainers must make concessions in order to obtain successful outcomes. Yet, many negotiators are unable to make material concessions because their opening position is too close to their expectation level. Adhering to this rule can be easily achieved by establishing an opening position that allows you to compromise and still reach your objective.

When negotiating contract price, government buyers should present an initial position below what they feel the ultimate price will be in order to be in the position to make concessions before agreeing on the final price. In contrast, government sellers should ask for more than what they expect to settle at so that the other side will be satisfied with a compromise that is still within the government's range of acceptable outcomes.

Examples

As Americans, we are also conditioned by our culture to expect flexibility during most types of negotiations. Accordingly, we can be penalized by having opening positions too close to our expectation level. Selling a home and buying a new car are examples of everyday transactions where the sellers are traditionally expected to settle at less than the asking price. For example, the home seller will generally have a more difficult time negotiating a $70,000 sale price when the asking price of the home is "listed" at $70,000. The reason for this negotiating difficulty is straightforward. Americans are culturally conditioned to expect the actual sale price for homes to be less than the asking price.

Automobile dealers have long practiced this bargaining technique by using "sticker prices" that are generally higher than what they expect their cars will actually sell for. This practice makes it easier for the salesperson to negotiate a better price for the dealership. But just as importantly, buying the car at a discount instills satisfaction in the buyer, who invariably feels that a "good deal" was obtained because the agreed upon price is below the sticker price.

Caution

A word of caution in applying this rule. If you give your side "too much room to compromise," your opening position could appear unreasonable to the other side. In these instances, the technique could even be counterproductive if it causes the contractor side to view the government as a "win/lose" negotiators. Guard against this predicament by supporting your opening position with valid reasons based on fact and reasonable judgments of what is likely to occur. In government contracting, the opening position is generally known as the government minimum or what the government side sincerely believes is the lowest fair and reasonable price.

5.3 Rule 3: Do Not Volunteer Weaknesses

Rationale

Although this rule is almost common sense, it is often overlooked because most Americans are candid and forthright by nature. The basic premise of this precept is that bargainers should not volunteer information that would weaken their negotiating position or enhance the bargaining position of the other side.

Negotiators need not be dishonest in order to comply with this rule. Honesty and ethical behavior are always paramount in any government negotiating session. Yet, there are many ways to respond to questions without telling falsehoods or volunteering information detrimental to your bargaining position. Adherence to this rule can often easily be accomplished by carefully wording statements or by avoiding a direct response to the question. For example, when a car owner is asked by a prospective buyer, "Why are you selling your car?", the seller can volunteer a weakness by saying, "My car is a gas guzzler." The seller not wanting to disclose the poor gas mileage can avoid revealing the weakness and still be honest by saying "I want to get another car" or "I just want to drive something different" or "I just want to sell my car."

Examples of Rule Violations

While Rule 3 appears to be a common sense position, examples of rule violations abound in everyday life --for instance, the prospective car buyer who willingly tells the salesperson that his or her old car is no longer running and that he or she needs a car for his or her job. Volunteering this information will make it more difficult for the car buyer to negotiate a good price.

Examples also abound in government contract negotiations where Rule 3 violations weakened the bargaining positions and sometimes resulted in needlessly higher contract prices. For instance,

- Without being asked, an Air Force engineer admitted during negotiations that the contractor proposal of $3.5 million was overly generous because the commanding general wanted the contract and $10 million in funding was available for the work. As a result of this admission, the contracting officer believed the negotiated contract price cost the government hundreds of thousands of dollars more than necessary.

- A Navy negotiator inadvertently divulged information on the extreme importance of completing a construction contract on time. Because of this admission, the contractor side correctly concluded that the government had a short deadline and would not have enough time to solicit other offers from competitive firms. This knowledge significantly weakened the government bargaining position, resulting in a higher than anticipated contract price.

- An attempt by a contractor negotiator to invoke pity on his firm by disclosing that the firm was behind on payments to subcontractors backfired when the government negotiator unfairly took advantage of this weakness. Unfortunately in response to this disclosure of weakness, the "win/lose" government negotiator was able to negotiate unreasonably low contractor overhead rates.

Summary   In summary, do not divulge information that hurts your bargaining position unless you cannot avoid the disclosure without being dishonest. In the absence of derogatory information, the other side is naturally more inclined to perceive strength and be unaware of the weaknesses in your position.

_____

5.4 Rule 4: Satisfy Non-price Needs

Rationale

Most negotiations will not end in agreement unless both sides are satisfied. This includes agreement on both price and non-price needs. Successful negotiators are able to identify the non-price needs of the other party and the ways to satisfy those needs. Yet, many negotiators enter negotiations with an awareness only of price issues facing both sides.

Never narrow down the objective of negotiations to just price issues. Look for non-price needs and the corresponding ways of satisfying the other party. These non-price needs are often not specified by the other side, but are nevertheless important. For example, the negotiation to buy a family-owned company includes more than just bargaining the sales price of the business. Other important non-price issues of the seller should also be addressed, such as the desire to protect the jobs of longtime employees or the retention of the family name on the business.

Non-price Needs in Government Contracting

Non-price needs are found in all government contract negotiations. For example, many contractors have cash flow problems that the government side can readily solve at little or no cost. Potential ways to satisfy this need include:

• Providing for partial deliveries with payment or acceptance for each shipment
• Earlier effective or start date for the contract
• Use of customary progress payments

Summary

In short, identify the many issues and underlying needs, other than price, that exist in every negotiation. Recognize that price is often not the only issue or even the single most important issue. And just as importantly, realize that the real bargaining has to do with satisfying both the price and non-price needs of the other side.

5.5 Rule 5: Use Concessions Wisely

Rationale	Since negotiations are essentially give-and-take sessions, successful negotiators are masters in the art of giving concessions. The way in which concessions are given has paramount influence on the outcome of the negotiation. To this end, the following important precepts of successful concession-making apply.
Ask for Something in Return	Never make a concession without getting, or at the very least, asking for a concession in return. Try to make the other side reciprocate when your side makes a concession. Linking concessions will facilitate more concessions from the other side by forcing concessions that otherwise would not have been made. Moreover, this technique will also enhance the value of your concessions. Negotiators, like most people in our society, generally put a higher value on something that requires a sacrifice on their part.
Small, Slow Concessions	Concede slowly and in small amounts. Large or quick concessions tend to unnecessarily raise the expectations of the other side. When this occurs, the overly generous concession becomes counterproductive to the negotiating process. Instead of bringing the parties closer together, the increased expectations of the other side result in the two sides being farther apart. Concessions quickly given or too large can also give the other side the impression that the concessions were not that important to the giver or that the concession giver is overly anxious for a settlement. In addition, big or quick concessions often result in more of a compromise than necessary.
Avoid Splitting the Difference	Just because someone wants to split the difference doesn't mean a fair settlement has been reached. Unless your negotiating objective has already been achieved when the other side offers to split, realize that you can get at least half of the difference and try to obtain an even larger concession. Remember that the one who offers to split the difference is in reality announcing a new position. When the other side refuses to split, the side making the offer cannot always easily retreat from their proposal. Do not auction or "ping pong" concessions by repetitive incremental concessions For example, the government should not keep increasing the profit rate in quick response to the contractor's offer to reduce the rate in similar increments.
Other Key Points of Concession Making	Concessions can be used to break an impasse, to win a corresponding concession from the other side, or to conclude an agreement. In general, concessions should be used only sparingly and after careful consideration. Moreover, it is often wise to call a recess to give your side the opportunity to examine the implications of a concession that falls outside the negotiation plan. Other key points of concession making in government contracting are: • Let the contractor make the first concession, when appropriate. • Attempt to get the contractor to concede on issues of major importance to your side instead of just conceding on minor or insignificant points.

- In contrast, make your first concessions on issues of minor importance to the government.

5.6 Rule 6: Put Pressure on the Other Side

Rationale

Because of the pressure inherent in every negotiation, success in negotiation stems in large part from the ability of bargainers to pressure the other side while at the same time limiting the pressure on themselves. Adherence to this rule can easily be accomplished by following some simple dictums which will reduce your stress while increasing the pressure on the other side.

Unknown Pressures Facing the Other Side

Believe in the unknown pressure facing the other side by realizing that there is more pressure on the other side than what is readily apparent. As stated earlier in Rule 1, bargainers have more information on their own position and, consequently, are naturally more aware of their own limitations than of the factors stressing the other side. Just believing that there are unknown pressures facing the other side will alleviate some of the pressure on your position.

Resist Artificial Pressures

Do not let artificial pressures, such as the perceived stature or the impressive credentials of the other side, increase the negotiating pressure on yourself. Nicely furnished offices in prestigious locations along with great sounding job titles should be of no help at negotiations unless the other bargainers are influenced by these fake pressures. For example, the fact that your bargaining counterpart is a company vice-president should not be any more stressful than if you were negotiating with the firm's janitor. I once worked for a company where all the salesmen were "vice-presidents" because the perceived stature of this job title often gave them leverage over many of the insecure buyers they negotiated with. Similarly, don't let certifications adorning walls or listed on calling cards intimidate you into thinking that owning the credentials makes that person an expert on crucial factors that can affect your position in the negotiation. Conversely, use artificial pressures of your own when negotiating.

Refer to Competitive Alternatives

In sole source negotiations, the government can put a great deal of pressure on the other side by referring to alternative choices or potential competition. Alternatives – such as canceling and resoliciting or buying in smaller quantities – always exist. Referring to potential competitors when they exist can also be effective. For example, a government negotiator could discuss changes in the requirement that could open the door to other competitors. Just the hint of potential competition often pressures the contractor to be more conciliatory and innovative in meeting the government needs.

5.7 Rule 7: Use the Power of Patience

Rationale

Although the virtue of patience sounds like motherhood and apple pie, negotiators need this important characteristic to help ensure success at the bargaining table. Practicing patience is often easier to say than to do because of the pressure inherent to every negotiation. The quicker the negotiations conclude, the sooner this natural pressure is relieved. Nonetheless, good negotiators use patience to their advantage to increase the stress on the other side while waiting for a better deal.

Cultural Barriers

American negotiators are generally more impatient compared to negotiators from other societies. Patience is even sometimes seen as an undesirable quality by the American culture. In contrast, societies known to value patience as a favorable virtue, such as the Japanese and Russians, produce negotiators whose patience enhances their bargaining skill. In fact, the Japanese believe that only a fool would quickly conclude a deal. Many winning American negotiators who value patience would agree with that assessment.

Benefits

Practicing patience also displays resolve or firmness in your position by demonstrating to the other side that you are not overly anxious for a settlement. The willingness to deliberately proceed through negotiations and, when necessary, delay the proceedings also dissipates the emotional feelings that surround certain issues. Quite often the extra negotiating time taken by patient government negotiators translates into thousands and even millions of dollars in additional concessions. In one such case, the government side negotiated a $40 million reduction on a $500 million contract by waiting for 2 days – instead of agreeing on price on the same day requested by of the program office.

Research has shown that the best deal for both sides takes time. Under a controlled environment where both sets of negotiators had access to the same facts, the quickest negotiations generally tended to have unbalanced or win/lose outcomes in favor of either the buyer or the seller. In contrast, the results of longer negotiation sessions for the same transaction tended to be more even. These results demonstrated that achieving balanced outcomes takes longer because both sides need time to explain their positions and develop ways to satisfy the other side.

5.8 Rule 8: Be Willing to Walk Away From or Back to Negotiations

Deadlocks Can't Always be Avoided

Deadlock cannot always be avoided and, in fact, is sometimes necessary when dealing with unfair or unreasonable parties. Even the best negotiators sometimes fail to come to a mutual agreement and experience this lose/lose outcome. However, good negotiators are neither afraid to walk away from bad deals nor too proud to return to the negotiation table once they realize a better deal could not have been obtained.

Government negotiators should have the resolve to walk away from what a reasonable person would consider to be a bad deal. Emotions or time constraints should not prevent objective thinking or acting in the best interests of the government. The willingness to deliberately deadlock when a fair deal cannot be obtained is extremely important because this attitude gives bargainers the resolve to credibly apply other bargaining techniques.

Returning After an Impasse

Successful negotiators should also have the ability to come back to the negotiation table after a deadlock. Once they learn that a better deal cannot be obtained in a timely fashion elsewhere, good negotiators do not let pride get in the way of renewing negotiations. Although it is usually better to let the other side make the first move after deadlock, you cannot be sure that will ultimately happen. But even when you make the first move, the other side will often welcome it because of the severe pressure on both parties caused by the deadlock.

Risks Associated with Walkouts

Walkouts or even the threat of walkouts may be used to advantage during the conduct of the negotiation, but not without some risk. The risk is that it may be very difficult to get the negotiation started again and back on track. If your walkout or threat to walkout leads to a concession, it is a successful technique. If the walkout fails, however and your position is weakened because an extreme technique did not work, reconciliation will be difficult . Whenever a negotiation conference has reached a point where you think you should terminate discussion and walk out, consider the impact your walkout will have. When you believe the other side will perceive the walkout as a clear indication they should be more flexible, then the walkout may be appropriate. When the walkout would be perceived as a win/lose ploy, then do not walk out unless your side has first tried everything else.

Strategies for Forestalling Walkouts

When you believe that a walkout by the contractor is imminent, it is probably advisable for you to try to forestall it. You could suggest a break or maybe even an overnight recess, with both parties having time to think things over and review their positions. Sometimes, it is even best to let the contractor walk out as a basis for emphasizing their unreasonableness. In any event, always remain cordial and express a willingness to reopen negotiations again if the contractor reconsidered. A walkout or threatened walkout should never force the government side to make unreasonable compromises.

5.9 Rule 9: Say It Right

Relevance	The time-worn axiom, "It's not what you say but how you say it," aptly applies to the way successful negotiators communicate to their counterparts on the other side. The importance of good interpersonal relationships between opposing negotiators on the outcome of negotiation cannot be overemphasized. The reason for this is simple: **Even the most generous offers may be refused when the feelings on the other side are ruffled.**
Importance of Word Choice	Use extreme care in your choice of words by using nonprovocative terms instead of their more provocative synonyms. For instance, use "resolute" instead of "stubborn" or "uninformed" rather than "stupid."
	Be polite and display respect for the contractor. Always state disagreements in a tactful and businesslike manner instead of responding in a way that may appear as a personal attack. For example, a response to an unacceptable offer might be "Thanks anyway but the government cannot accept that," instead of a personal remark such as "That offer is an insult to my intelligence." Using discourteous or disrespectful language only upsets the other side and makes it that much harder to obtain good deals.
Example of a Rule Violation	A real-life example of the damage attributable to a "Say It Right" violation occurred when the government made a true but derogatory opening remark about a member of the contractor team. Since this was said at the start of bargaining, an adversarial tone was thus set for the remainder of the negotiation. The offended contractor resisted even the most reasonable requests, not because of the fairness or logic involved but because of the hurt feelings caused by the damaging remark.
Key Points	Make disagreements as courteous as possible by not personalizing contentious issues. A good way to do this is to never disagree using personal pronouns, such as you, me, or I. Good negotiators only use personal pronouns when they agree with the position of the other side.
	Along with the choice of words, the tone of voice is important. Be careful not to sound insincere or overly eager for a settlement; Speak in a voice that projects strength and confidence, rather than sounding tentative. Moreover, do not chance slighting the other side by saying things in a condescending or angry tone of voice.
	Finally, do not say anything that has even a remote chance of being controversial if: • It doesn't help the government position, or • It does not have a bearing on the negotiation.

Negotiators often make innocuous comments that they themselves do not find offensive. However, they may inadvertently upset individuals who are sensitive about the subject. An illustration of this is the seemingly inoffensive statement: "Isn't it great that the Cubs won." Even this innocuous remark could have a negative effect if the negotiator on the other side just does not like the Cubs. **Remember "Say it Right" violations occur even when you have no intention of being disrespectful or provoking the other side.** The test on whether or not this rule has been violated is how the other side perceives it.

Say It Right Checklist

You can use the following table as a checklist of ways to "Say It Right":

Say it Right Checklist	
	Sell yourself and your ideas. Since you are in actuality selling your negotiating position, act as polite and cordial as would a persuasive salesperson.
	Never lie or say anything dishonest.
	Only use personal pronouns (such as "you", "I", "we") when you agree with the other side. Avoid personal pronouns when you disagree.
	Don't embarrass the other side by being negative when discussing circumstances relating to your negotiating counterparts.
	Be cautious about expressing unrelated opinions. Chances are that others will disagree with these opinions more often than they will agree.
	Be sensitive to the other side and show interest in their views.
	Think before you speak and try to anticipate possible negative reactions.
	Keep it simple. Bargainers generally will not agree to things they don't understand.
	Be calm and don't lose your temper even when the other side commits "Say It Right" violations and provokes you.
	Deal from strength, use your strong points - be confident.
	Be personal, but businesslike. Learn names and use them, but be cautious about addressing the other side on a first-name basis.
	Continue to be polite even when the other side is rude or provocative.

79

5.10 Rule 10: Be Prepared

Importance of Preparation

The motto of scouting, "Be Prepared," applies to the conduct of successful negotiations. No amount of experience, skill, or persuasion on the part of the negotiator can fully compensate for the absence of preparation. Simply put, successful negotiators are generally the most prepared negotiators. Moreover, none of these bargaining rules can be entirely effective without adherence to this rule.

Sellers are usually more prepared than buyers, and this gives contractors an important advantage in most bargaining sessions. Although members of the contractor side may not spend any more time on this contract than the government, the cumulative preparation time they have spent selling the same product over and over again to commercial buyers often gives them an edge over individual buyers. Moreover, contractors usually know more about their relatively unique product because it is the reason they are in business and, afterall, they produce it and may have even invented the deliverable. Adequate preparation by the government side is necessary to offset this significant negotiating edge.

Characteristics of Adequate Preparation

Adequate preparation for most negotiations includes a careful study of the strengths and weaknesses of both positions along with a study of the needs of the other party and the ways to satisfy those needs. Successful negotiators realize that a relatively small amount of preparation in these areas is well worth the effort. In fact, no other aspect of negotiation continually pays better returns than preparing for the upcoming bargaining session. Conversely, poor preparation adversely affects your side way out of proportion to the time saved. Since there is just no substitute for good preparation, you should never negotiate an issue unless you are adequately prepared.

5.11 Summary

Successful Negotiations

The ability to negotiate successfully is possessed by people with varying personalities, from all walks of life, and under a multitude of differing bargaining conditions. Success at negotiations is determined as much by the skill of the negotiator as the circumstances surrounding the bargaining session. Although different bargainers adhere to those techniques that work for them, most winning negotiators appear to have certain characteristics in common. Hopefully, you too will be able to improve your chances for negotiating success by applying these bargaining techniques to your professional bargaining sessions.

CHAPTER 6: NEGOTIATION TACTICS

Learning
Objectives

At the end of this chapter you will be able to:

Primary Learning Objective
Select and apply tactics, recognize tactics used by the other party, and counter win/lose tactics used by the other party.

Classroom Learning Objective 6/1
Recognize and apply win/win tactics.

Classroom Learning Objective 6/2
Recognize appropriate times to use win/lose tactics.

Classroom Learning Objective 6/3
Recognize tactics used by the other party.

Classroom Learning Objective 6/4
Counter win/lose tactics used by the other party.

Contents and Procedures

6.0 Introduction

Negotiation Tactics Defined

Negotiators use a variety of tactics or ploys in attempting to achieve their bargaining aims. Since most bargaining ploys are deceptive in nature, tactics usually tend to be win/lose in orientation. Accordingly, the application of win/lose tactics is generally not recommended in government contract negotiations because these tactics often facilitate win/lose outcomes.

Nevertheless, there are important reasons to study the tactics encountered most often in government contract negotiations. First, by identifying a tactic for what it really is, we can lessen the value of the tactic as a bargaining ploy that benefits the other side. Because just recognizing a tactic reduces its effectiveness, tactic identification becomes a universal countermeasure that applies to all tactics. Second, an understanding of the many different bargaining devices gives the skilled negotiator greater opportunities for success. Precise countermeasures can be applied against win/lose tactics. And finally, win/win tactics can be used to facilitate win/win bargaining objectives. In some instances, even win/lose tactics can sometimes be employed against win/lose negotiators to achieve win/win outcomes.

Although there is an endless array of different negotiation tactics, each used in many different variations, this chapter will focus on the bargaining ploys most commonly encountered in government contract negotiations and on their corresponding countermeasures. Keep in mind that any tactic can be modified or used in conjunction with other tactics, depending on the unique circumstances surrounding every bargaining session. Moreover, there are many more countermeasures than the ones listed in the text. But there is a universal countermeasure which applies to every tactic. Just by recognizing a tactic for what it really is --a bargaining ploy --reduces or eliminates its effectiveness.

84

6.1 Win/Lose Tactics

Introduction The following tactics are generally considered win/lose tactics because they represent bargaining ploys or ways to facilitate negotiation objectives by deceiving the other side. Because of the inherently dishonest nature of these win/lose tactics, their application is generally not recommended for negotiators seeking win/win outcomes. Nevertheless, by understanding the win/lose tactics, win/win negotiators will be better able to defend against their successful application. In addition, the employment of some win/lose tactics by win/win negotiators may sometimes be desirable when facing win/lose bargainers.

Funny Money Description. Bargainers use diversionary words and symbols to represent true monetary values during the negotiations.

Purpose. Funny money can hide the actual dollar amount. Monetary symbols like profit rates, indirect cost percentages, and price per pound distract attention from determining the true cost dollar value. The recipient of the tactic can be lulled into accepting amounts that are different than what would have been the case had actual dollar amounts been used instead of funny money versions. A common application of this tactic by contractors is to use profit percentages to hide the expected true dollar amount of profit.

Countermeasure. Translate all funny money terms to their actual monetary equivalent. For example, when negotiating profit rates, calculate the dollar value represented by the percentage.

Surprise Description. Negotiators may introduce an unexpected behavior, issue, or goal at an unexpected point in the proceedings. This tactic often invokes a non-spontaneous event to surprise or shock the other side, such as a planned emotional outburst. A good example of this tactic occurred when the Soviet Premier, Nikita Kruschev, pounded his shoe on the speaker's podium at the United Nations. Since the shoe used by Nikita for this outburst was not one of the shoes he was wearing, we can safely conclude that this surprise tactic was planned.

Purpose. If the other party has not anticipated the surprise, they will not have had time to formulate counter rationales or counterbalancing concessions. Consequently, the user may be able to win the objective without having to yield anything. The apparent shock or surprise is also used to elicit an emotional response from the other side that facilitates the user's objectives.

Countermeasure. Call a caucus or somehow delay a response. Do not respond until you are prepared. Do not get emotional or flustered.

Blanketing

Description. Negotiators using this tactic ask for everything at once ("blanketing" the other side) by opening the negotiation with all their demands at once. Although this is generally a win/lose ploy, the tactic can be used in a win/win mode when the intention of the user is to be up front and open by putting all the issues on the table at the onset of negotiations.

Purpose. The user of this tactic hopes that the other side will be overwhelmed with the extent of all the demands and concede on the more important issues.

Countermeasure. Before making any concessions, prioritize the issues to determine what is really essential to the other side and how important the issue is to the government.

Undermining

Description. The bargainer using this tactic attempts to put the other side on the defensive by use of threats, insults, or ultimatums. Although this win/lose tactic often backfires because most people resent verbal attacks, the tactic can sometimes be effective when used against easily intimidated negotiators.

Purpose. The negotiator using this risky tactic hopes to gain concessions by bullying the other side. Some contractor negotiators have tried to lower the confidence of the government by making negative comments about the incompetence of government personnel and their frustration with the "red tape" involved in selling to federal agencies.

Countermeasure. There are several countermeasures to this win/lose tactic:

- If the threat is unethical, unlawful, or immoral, state that you intend to report the threat to the proper authorities, such as the other side's superiors.

- Explain the long-range risks and costs that would result if the contractor side decides to carry out the threat.

- Play ignorant by failing to understand the threat and go on to the next issue.

- Do not become shaken or emotional when this tactic takes the form of an insult. Insist on respect but continue to be businesslike and polite.

Silence

Description. A party using this tactic does not say anything about a negotiation point, hoping that the issue does not come up. If the negotiation point is mentioned, the user of this tactic remains silent or avoids the topic by talking about something else.

Purpose. This tactic is generally used when negotiators do not want to disclose weaknesses in their position. For example, a contractor trying to sell unwarranted parts to the government would not want to mention the fact that the parts do not have warranties. The tactic is also used when bargainers want to obtain information by letting the other side do the talking. In this case, some negotiators feel obligated to talk and reveal information on their position when the other side is deliberately silent. Sometimes these negotiators will even end up talking themselves into accepting the other side's positions.

Countermeasure. Ask persistent and effective questions to uncover the avoided topic.

Feinting

Description. Negotiators employing this tactic use true, but misleading statements or behavior.

Purpose. Feinting gives the other side a false impression or deceives the other side into believing something that is not true. For example, a Navy contractor "feinted" by telling the government negotiator that the construction project had already begun when only some minor tree clearing had taken place. In fact, the contractor was unable to start construction because the earth-moving equipment needed was still being used on another job.

Countermeasure. Ask probing questions to determine the real situation or bring out the hidden topic.

Limited Authority

Description. Bargainers using this tactic claim they do not have the authority to negotiate a certain issue.

Purpose. Negotiating with limited authority is used to find out the limits of the other side's position without committing your side. For example, contractors will sometimes use this tactic to find out what the government will pay without stating their price, by claiming that their negotiators do not have final authority on price.

Countermeasure. Offer to negotiate with the authority figure. This tactic can even be preempted by determining at the start of negotiations if there are any limitations on the authority of the negotiator for the other side.

Apparent Withdrawal

Description. Bargainers break off negotiations with the unannounced intention of resuming bargaining later. Real-life examples of this occurred after the Arab oil embargo when some oil companies used "apparent withdrawal" because the government offer was often less than the rapidly increasing market price for oil. However, these oil companies knew they would have to resume bargaining because of a legal requirement to supply oil to the government.

Purpose. This tactic is accomplished to let the other side know how serious you are on a particular issue that is very important to your side. However, the apparent withdrawal can be a dangerous device because there is always a significant risk that the other side will not want to resume negotiations again. The best time for using this tactic is when every other attempt to move the other side on an important and vital point has been unsuccessful.

Countermeasure. Wait out the other side until they request that the bargaining session be resumed.

Deadline

Description. Negotiators establish arbitrary time limits or deadlines to force deals and make things happen. The deadline tactic is frequently used by contractors, who establish short time limits by claiming that the deal must be consummated by a certain time or conditions disadvantageous to the government, such as price increases will become present.

Purpose. Time limits create pressure on the other side to settle. In some cases, the government side has been able to secure timely deals by imposing settlement deadlines on contractors. However, deadlines can also be used to rush one of the parties into quick and possibly unfavorable agreements. Time limits or threats of a deadline can also be used to enhance bargaining positions. Examples of arbitrary deadlines are expiration dates for contract award, dates for budget passage, or price increase dates.

Countermeasure. Be skeptical of deadlines. Generally, short time limits indicate the application of this tactic. Since deadlines are generally arbitrary and can be extended, countermeasures include:

- Bargaining for more time or for an extension

- Asking the contractor to prove the deadline is real

- Purposely missing the deadline

Good Guy/ Bad Guy

Description. This tactic involves role playing by members of the negotiating team. One member plays an easy-going "good guy" role while another team member role plays the hard-core or difficult "bad guy" bargainer. The "bad guy" may even take an extreme position which sometimes involves a serious threat to the other party.

Purpose. The "good guy" position is basically the same position the other team is striving for. The "good guy" attempts to convince the other side that the only alternative to the "bad guy" position is accepting the "good guy" outcome.

In some actual cases, the contracting officer played the "bad guy" and refused to budge on any issues. After the contracting officer left the bargaining session, the contractor then became eager to quickly settle with the other government negotiator role-playing the "good guy". This is the very type of win/lose bargaining ploy that the government negotiators should generally avoid.

Countermeasure. Ignore the extreme position and confine your bargaining to the "good guy" position with effective responses and points. If the "bad guy" is too disruptive, tell the other party to remove the "bad guy" or you will break off negotiations.

Invoking Fake Competition	Description. Negotiators using this tactic openly and blatantly praise the benefits of false alternative choices which compete against the position of the other side.
	Purpose. Referring to bogus competition can be very effective because this pressures the other side. The perception of better alternatives often causes the other side to doubt the reasonableness of their position. In some real-life instances, the contractor side has been able to invoke "bogus competition" by referring to *non-existent* higher prices paid by other customers that do not exist.
	Countermeasure. Since this tactic is often used when no valid alternatives are available, question why bargaining is even taking place when the alternatives or competition are so good.
Wet Noodle	Description. Negotiators using this tactic are difficult to pin down on any issue because they give qualified or noncommittal responses.
	Purpose. Users of this tactic frequently do not want to make concessions or commitments.
	Countermeasure. Force a firm response from the other side before moving on to another issue.
Take it or Leave it	Description. This tactic is being used when the other side signals that agreement is expected without negotiation or any further bargaining, such as "I crossed out two items in the contract--sign here," or "My best offer is on the table and I have no room to compromise further."
	Purpose. The user wants to dictate the outcome by making the other side feel they are expected to accept (or reject) the offer at face value without further negotiation.
	Countermeasure. There are three effective countermeasures to this tactic. First, ignore the tactic by insisting that everything is negotiable. Indeed, even the prices of grocery items are negotiated in many countries around the world unless the buyer wants to pay more than the market price. Secondly, counter by obtaining other, non-price concessions. Finally, apply the "apparent withdrawal" tactic by ending the bargaining session and walking out.
Fait Accompli	Description: Fait accompli is presenting the other party with a completed action, insisting they have little or no choice but to accept it.
	Purpose. The user hopes the other side will accept the proposal because the action has already been completed. For example, the contractor presents the government with an unsigned written contract expecting the government to sign the agreement without negotiation.
	Countermeasure. Insist that everything is negotiable and that your side always intended to bargain for the issue.

Bogey

Description. Bargainers using this tactic blame their negotiating positions on third parties or situations beyond their control, such as limited funding. Any excuse in the world can be used for this tactic as long as the reasons given are beyond the control of the negotiator.

Purpose. Bargainers using the tactic may escape responsibility for their position since the "bogey" is supposedly beyond their control. Because of this lack of accountability, the tactic tends to lower expectations without getting the other side upset with the negotiator.

Countermeasure. Bogey countermeasures include:

- Stand firm and insist on your position.
- Offer to bargain with the "bogey" when the excuse is a third party.
- Counter the bogey directly, such as proposing alternative financing when limited budgets are used as the excuse.

Crunch

Description. Regardless of the generosity of the proposal, the user of this tactic is never satisfied and responds in words to the effect: "You have to do better than that," or "That is not good enough."

Purpose. This win/lose tactic often lowers expectations because the other side begins to doubt the reasonableness of their own position. The tactic may also engender appreciation when the other party feels grateful for a second chance.

Countermeasure. Keep the burden of proof on the other side by asking them to justify the crunch.

Decoy

Description. Bargainers place apparent importance on a straw issue whose outcome is really not that important to them. This technique also involves fabricating issues or blowing minor issues out of proportion, only to concede after a lengthy discussions. A variation of this tactic occurs when the contractor deliberately inflates the proposal price through detectable errors that the government can be expected to find.

Purpose. Users have the intention of trading the decoy for a concession of value. When effectively applied, this strategy enables the user to obtain a valuable concession without giving up anything important in return. For example, the contractor will pretend to grudgingly concede on the straw issue of a price estimating error, but will not make other concessions on issues important to their side.

Countermeasure. Decoy counter measures include:

- Concede the straw issue and hold out for a trade of value.

- Call their bluff by challenging the validity of the issue.

Legitimacy

Description. Legitimacy involves the use of commonly accepted standards, past practice, official policy, or written documents to support a bargaining position. For example, contractors often use results of prior negotiations and published price lists to confer legitimacy on their proposals.

Purpose. By conveying legitimacy on a position, the bargainer hopes to reduce or eliminate negotiations on that issue because many people are reluctant to challenge the status quo or question a position that is supported by an official document.

Countermeasure. Ignore the tactic and insist that everything is negotiable. For example, a skilled government negotiator refused to accept "official price lists" and bargained far better prices for the government.

6.2 Win/Win Tactics

Introduction

The following tactics are generally win/win in nature. Since these tactics are used to facilitate win/win outcomes, countermeasures to win/win tactics are generally not appropriate. However, even win/win tactics can be abused and used as win/lose bargaining ploys by win/lose negotiators. Counters to win/lose use are listed with each tactic throughout this section.

Forbearance

Description. Forbearance occurs when both sides agree to disagree and move on to the next issue without making a commitment one way or the other.

Purpose. When both sides disagree on an issue, using this tactic can prevent the negotiation from bogging down on areas of disagreement. Instead, the bargainers search for areas each party can agree on. Delaying agreement efforts can also give each side more time to view the unresolved issues in a different light.

Counter to Win/Lose Use. Offer to trade the areas of disagreement, whereby one side accepts a concession in exchange for an equal concession by the other side.

Questioning

Description. This tactic involves the use of questions to move the negotiations along.

Purpose. The negotiator asks questions for many useful purposes, including:

- Obtaining additional facts or specific information on the other side's position, such as the contractor's range for settlement.
- Seeking a specific response, such as "What is the best you can do?"
- Giving information by using questions that begin with "Did you consider . .?"
- Breaking impasses using questions such as, "Why...?" or "Suppose. . .?"
- Assisting the other side in reaching agreement with questions such as, "When can you start work?" Such questions can often precipitate a settlement.

Some win/lose negotiators wanting to determine the available funding for government construction contracts have used this tactic by asking questions on resource requirements, such as "How many cubic yards of concrete are we talking about," or "How long do you think this job will take?". If the answers to these questions are forthcoming, the contractor may be able to convert quantities or job length into a good approximation of the government position.

Counter to Win/Lose Use. When you suspect "questioning" is stemming from the win/lose perspective, counter by either not answering the question, responding with another question, or just listening.

Trial Balloon	Description. Negotiators using a trial balloon present the other side with options by prefacing offers with "what if . . . .". Without committing the user, issues are brought up for discussion politely, giving the other side refusal or acceptance options. For example, the government side might say, "How would the contractor feel about this alternative?"
	Purpose. Using this tactic allows each side to bounce off ideas for win/win solutions. "Trial balloons" are proposed in such a way that the other party is encouraged to offer alternative solutions.
	Counter to Win/Lose Use. When in doubt about the acceptability of a trial balloon, take enough time to formulate a response. "What ifs" sometimes require time to answer and generally cannot be analyzed on the spot.
Alternative Positions	Description. Another win/win tactic is offering alternative positions at the same time during the bargaining session.
	Purpose. The other side has the opportunity to select options or alternative courses of action most favorable to their position, thus minimizing any adverse consequences of not obtaining agreement on the primary position of the other party. Moreover, the selection itself gives the other side ownership in the solution.
	Counter to Win/Lose Use. Spend enough time to thoroughly analyze the merits and drawbacks of every option before making your selection. Avoid accepting a false dilemma because there may be other alternatives. The pros and cons of each alternative position may not be readily apparent.
Acceptance Time	Description. Instead of forcing a quick decision, a negotiator may deliberately give the other side enough time to grasp proposals or ideas by suggesting a break in negotiations.
	Purpose. Negotiators, like people in general, need time to accept something new or different.
	Counter to Win/Lose Use. Do not take too much time to decide because the momentum could be lost for quick agreement. Too much time could also allow the other side to make changes to their position.
Brainstorming	Description. The negotiator using this tactic thinks out loud and openly discusses many ideas with the other side, such as possible solutions or concessions which would resolve the issues.
	Purpose. When sincere in its approach, brainstorming can be a useful tactic to identify all the needs (including the hidden non-price issues and underlying needs of the other side).
	Counter to Win/Lose Use. The win/lose counter is to simply say nothing and listen.

Salami

Description. The negotiator using this tactic makes demands one demand at a time (or bit by bit as when cutting salami) rather than requesting everything all at once.

Purpose. Using this tactic gives the win/win negotiator the opportunity to fully explain and sell each position before moving on to another issue. The other side does not fully realize how many demands are going to be made and, consequently, may be more receptive to early concessions. Salami is also used by negotiators to "get a foot in the door" and try for a small piece of the action, rather than attempting to negotiate for the entire pie.

Counter to Win/Lose Use. When you suspect the other side is win/lose, the countermeasure for salami is making the other party specify all their demands before making the first concession. Refuse piecemeal settlements.

Bracketing

Description. This tactic occurs when a negotiator narrows down the issues to determine what issues are essential to the other side. Bracketing is often used as a countermeasure to the "blanketing" tactic.

Purpose. The bargainer uses bracketing to find out what the other side would be willing to take, leaving aside the unimportant or extraneous issues.

Counter to Win/Lose Use. Countermeasures include qualified or non-committal responses. Make sure the critical brackets include your issues.

6.3 Summary

Summary

Negotiation tactics are used for the purpose of obtaining bargaining objectives. Win/lose negotiation tactics are generally ploys or deceptions used to gain advantage by deceiving the other side. Accordingly, the application of win/lose tactics is generally not recommended in government contract negotiations. However, win/win tactics should be used to facilitate win/win outcomes. Win/lose tactics can even be used under exceptional circumstances against win/lose negotiators to achieve win/win outcomes.

An understanding of the most commonly used tactics found in government contract negotiations also helps the win/win negotiator successfully counter win/lose bargaining ploys. The universal countermeasure to all such tactics is simply identifying the tactic for what it really is, namely, a negotiation ploy. The recognition of win/lose tactics will reduce, if not completely eliminate, the effectiveness of the tactic as a successful negotiation device.

CHAPTER 7: NONVERBAL NEGOTIATING

Learning Objectives

At the end of this chapter you will be able to:

Primary Learning Objective (PLO)
Recognize and interpret nonverbal cues used by participants (including self).
Use nonverbal messages.

Classroom Learning Objective 7/1
Explain importance of nonverbals in negotiations.

Classroom Learning Objective 7/2
Describe the role of body language in negotiating.

Classroom Learning Objective 7/3
Describe the role of physical environment in negotiating.

Classroom Learning Objective 7/4
Describe the role of personal appearance in negotiating.

Classroom Learning Objective 7/5
Describe the role of human voice and the handshake in negotiating.

Contents and Procedures

7.0 Chapter Overview

Communication is More Than Verbal

Since negotiation is defined as **"a <u>communication</u> process whereby both parties attempt to reach agreement on a matter of common concern,"** good negotiators must also be good communicators. Yet, many negotiators think of communication only as verbal exchanges in speech or writing. But verbal formulations account for only a small portion of the messages people send and receive. Scientific research has shown that between 70 and 90 percent of the entire spectrum of all communication is of the nonverbal variety.[1] Consequently, government negotiators should be aware of the different forms of nonverbal messages they are likely to encounter during bargaining sessions.

Although most people are not fully aware of other ways to communicate besides the traditional verbal methods of using the written or spoken word, without realizing it these same people continually send and receive nonverbal messages. This phenomenon is continually demonstrated in my class when students do not respond to the question, "Who is your favorite nonverbal communicator?" However, when the question is restated to say "Who is your favorite actor or model?" most students readily voice their preference. Many individuals simply do not realize that the primary determinant to success in acting or modeling is the ability to communicate nonverbally. After all, anyone can read script or pose--it is the rare ability to send just the right nonverbal messages that separates the very best from the very worst performers.

---

[1]For the purposes of this book, verbal communication means communication with words whether spoken or written.

7.1 Recognize Nonverbal Communication and its Importance in Negotiation

Importance of Nonverbals

The importance of nonverbals is becoming more and more evident in our society. Consumer behavior experts are used by businesses to detect good sales prospects through nonverbal buying habits. In the courtroom, attorneys for both sides rely on nonverbal experts to determine jury selections. Juries themselves often rely on nonverbal cues given by defendants and witnesses to determine legal verdicts. In every walk of life, people continually rely on nonverbal messages to form their opinions of situations and of other individuals, because the great majority of our daily intercourse is of the nonverbal variety.

A good understanding of nonverbal messages will always be to our benefit during negotiations. Bargainers skilled at interpreting nonverbals will be able to glean useful information from the other side. An awareness of nonverbal communication modes may also prevent government negotiators from harming their own bargaining position by inadvertently sending nonverbal signals that disclose confidential information or weaknesses in their bargaining position.

Bargainers who look only for the overt meanings of verbal signals by focusing on what they see in writing or what they hear in human speech, miss many important messages. In contrast, negotiators with an awareness of both nonverbal and verbal messages have an important edge.

Illustration 1 shows two negotiation teams. The nonverbal messages indicated by their body postures, facial gestures, and appearance convincingly demonstrate the attitudes of each side. The team on the right transmits nonverbals exuding confidence and success. In contrast, the nonverbals of the team on the left convey negative attitudes and other unflattering characteristics. The nonverbals of which side exhibit the greatest likelihood for bargaining success and a win/win negotiation style? Which side would you prefer to emulate?

Illustration 1
Nonverbal
Negotiating

Which side is winning?

Definitions

Nonverbals consist of all forms of communication that are not derived from the language we speak or write. When communicating in a nonverbal manner, we reveal ourselves not in what we say, but in everything we do. Scientific research in the area has identified over a dozen different nonverbal specialties, including:

- Kinesis (body language) is the study of nonverbal messages indicated by body movements, gestures, and posture.

- Oculesics (eye behavior) examines communication sent by the movement of the human eye, such as looking away.

- Haptics (touching behavior) studies the messages conveyed by the way people touch each other, such as in handshaking.

- Vocalics (study of sound) explores the communication sent by inflections of the voice and nonverbal sounds, such as laughter.

- Proxemics (study of space and distance) studies the messages sent by the physical surrounding and the distance or proximity of people to each other.

Different Nonverbal Messages

Nonverbals can be communicated as conscious or subliminal messages in either a deliberate or an involuntary manner.

Conscious and deliberate nonverbals

Senders of conscious nonverbals are deliberately trying to communicate. For example, the individual extending a hug wants to convey friendship. Similarly, a person could deliberately pat someone on the back to communicate support.

Most receivers of conscious nonverbal communication are aware of the meaning intended by the sender. The receiver of a hug, for instance, generally realizes that the message is a sign of friendship.

Subliminal nonverbals

Subliminal messages are communicated to the subconscious mind of the receiver. Receivers of subliminal messages are not consciously aware of the message. Gut reactions are frequently based upon the subconscious reading of subliminal nonverbals, so we should not ignore them when forming opinions.

Modern society provides us with many examples of subliminal nonverbals. The symbols of authority conveyed by the wearing of police and military uniforms are subliminally communicated. Personal appearance transmits both conscious and subconscious messages; well-dressed executives project success and credibility, while poorly dressed images transmit subliminal messages denoting failure and lack of credibility.

Although subliminals do not create awareness on the conscious level, the receiver is still influenced by the communication. In fact, subconscious communication often has a more powerful impact than conscious messages.

The advertising world is replete with examples of the value of subliminal nonverbal messages. Young, beautiful people are often seen in advertisements to communicate the subconscious message that the advertised product is associated with youth and beauty (and is therefore better). Companies also pay large sums of money to have their products appear in movies. While these appearances are not typical product advertisements, the mere association of the product with the movie transmits subliminal messages that will influence viewers to prefer the product.

Involuntary nonverbals

Most nonverbal messages are sent involuntarily. Although the preceding examples illustrated deliberate nonverbal communication by the advertising world, nonverbal negotiators are often not aware when they communicate with nonverbals.

The involuntary nature of nonverbal communication is particularly evident in the area of body language. People unintentionally convey nonverbal signals by their facial expressions, gestures, and body postures. For example, people telling falsehoods often involuntarily send nonverbal messages indicated by frequent eye blinking. Because involuntary nonverbals represent unplanned physical responses, this communication form tends to be particularly revealing and more honest than verbal communication or even conscious nonverbal messages.

Sometimes nonverbals cannot be accurately interpreted because the messages have multiple meanings. For instance, the meaning of a yawn may be either lack of interest or actual physical fatigue. Similarly, rapid eye blinking might indicate deceit or just poor-fitting contact lenses. Nevertheless, nonverbals can be relied on to a great extent because even the spoken and written word is often ambiguous. However, interpreting nonverbal messages is often more difficult because so many nonverbals are transmitted to the subconscious mind. Look for patterns of behavior that correlate with each other to obtain more accurate interpretations of nonverbal messages.

Cultural Influences	The meanings of the same nonverbal can be different in other societies. Just as the same sounding word has different interpretation when spoken in other languages, identical nonverbals are sometimes interpreted in different ways by other cultures. For example, while maintaining eye contact when communicating in person is acceptable in our society, eye contact in other societies can be seen as offensive.
Importance of Nonverbals in Negotiations	An awareness of nonverbal communication is particularly important in negotiations because the greater honesty of the nonverbals can be used to verify the verbal message. Comparisons between the stated word and the nonverbal signal can disclose inconsistencies between the two different kinds of communication. Negotiators can make a better impression by sending nonverbal and verbal messages that do not conflict. The types of nonverbal communication typically found in the bargaining setting most helpful to negotiators consist of body language, the physical environment, personal appearance, voice sounds, and the handshake.

7.2 Recognize How Body Language Sends Nonverbal Messages

Body Language   The nonverbal area of body language examines the meaning of facial expressions along with the different postures and gestures of the various parts of the human body. Research on the subject has catalogued 135 distinct gestures and expressions of the face, head, and body. Eighty of these expressions were face and head gestures, including nine different ways of smiling.

Understanding body expressions is tremendously important for the negotiator because physical manifestations transmit important messages that either validate or conflict with verbal communication. Most physical expressions consist of involuntary reactions which communicate messages that the originator inadvertently sends. As mentioned earlier, excessive blinking often serves as a lie detector to indicate dishonesty.

Even the interpretation of conscious expressions are helpful when the physical display discloses more than what the sender intended. For example, showing displeasure over a negotiating position may also reveal a personal dislike for the other side. Similarly, a deliberate show of anticipation may inadvertently disclose an overeagerness to settle.

Body language indicates varying attitudes of the originator. Quite frequently, multiple expressions conveying the same meaning are exhibited at the same time. These simultaneous physical signals reinforce each other and may reduce ambiguity surrounding the message. For example, eagerness is often exhibited with the simultaneous physical displays of excessive smiling along with frequent nodding of the head.

The common attitudes communicated nonverbally during negotiations can be grouped into the two broad classifications of positive attitudes and negative attitudes.

Positive Attitudes   Positive attitudes interpreted from common body expressions may be useful in facilitating win/win strategies. They include the attitudes listed below.

Confidence is often exhibited by the following nonverbal signals:

- Hands in pocket with thumbs out
- Hands on lapel of coat
- Steepled fingers or hands
- Good body posture, such as square shoulders and a straight back
- Hands on hips

Interest may be exhibited by the following nonverbals which are often done simultaneously:

- Tilted head toward speaker
- Sitting on edge of chair
- Upper body leaning in sprinter's position
- Eyes focused on speaker

Evaluation gestures are frequently indicated by the following signs, some of which are accomplished together:

- Peering out over eyeglasses
- Pipe smoker gesture with chin cupped between thumb and fingers (classic example is Rodan sculpture "The Thinker.")
- Putting hands to bridge of nose
- Stroking chin

Eagerness is often demonstrated by the following gestures:

- Rubbing hands together
- Smiling excessively
- Frequent nodding of the head

Negative Attitudes

Common negative attitudes conveyed by body expressions include the nonverbals listed below.

Deception or dishonesty is often demonstrated by the following signs:

- Frequent eye blinking
- Hand covering mouth while speaking
- Looking away while speaking
- Quick sideways glances

Defensiveness may be indicated by the following nonverbals:

- Arms crossed high on chest
- Crossed legs
- Pointing index finger

Insecurity is often exhibited in the following manner:

- Hands completely in pocket
- Constant fidgeting
- Chewing pencil or biting fingernails
- Hand wringing

Frustration is frequently shown by the following nonverbal mannerisms:

- Tightness of jaw
- Rubbing back of neck
- Drawing brows together

Boredom or indifference is generally displayed in the following manner:

- Eyes not focused at speaker or looking elsewhere
- Head in hand
- Sloppy or informal body posture
- Preoccupation with something else

7.3 Recognize How the Physical Environment Sends Nonverbal Messages

Physical Environment	The physical environment transmits nonverbal communication that is extremely important to negotiators. An understanding of the nonverbal messages transmitted from seating arrangements and facilities can give bargainers a big edge in negotiations.
Seating Arrangements	Seating arrangements convey powerful nonverbal messages. They include the size and shape of the bargaining tables and the seating location of the chief negotiator.
Bargaining Table Configuration	Although there is no "standard" table configuration for every negotiation session, the way the bargaining tables are arranged transmits important conscious and subliminal messages. It is worth remembering that the Paris peace negotiation to end the Vietnam War were delayed for almost a year over negotiations on the shape of the bargaining table.
	The bargaining table configurations in Illustration 2 convey different messages. Arrangement A is a typical configuration with two parties on opposite sides of the table facing each other. Arrangement B may tend to give one side an advantage over the other because the arrangement suggests only one important figure at the end of the vertical extension. The distance between the tables in Arrangement C shows a need for "space" between the two sides, which could mean more formality or less trust. Finally, Arrangement D may be the most conducive to win/win negotiations because the round shape is usually associated with equality.
	The best table arrangement for any negotiation depends on the situation. However, win/win negotiation attitudes can be promoted with table configurations that convey trust. In contrast, win/lose attitudes are created by table settings that communicate disparity or mistrust between the two sides.
Position of Chief Negotiator	The physical position of the lead negotiator is generally at the center of the negotiation team. The central position conveys a message of authority and sends an image of a unified bargaining team. For example, the American President (as the most powerful person in the U.S. government) will be always be seen seated at the center of every conference table.
	Besides sending negative nonverbals, positioning the chief negotiator somewhere other than the center seat also has adverse practical consequences.

Some members may not be able to whisper advice, give cues, or pass notes when the principal negotiator is at an end position. The ideal place for the chief negotiator in each arrangement shown in the illustration is the middle seat flanked by team members on either side.

**Illustration 2
Bargaining
Table
Configuration**

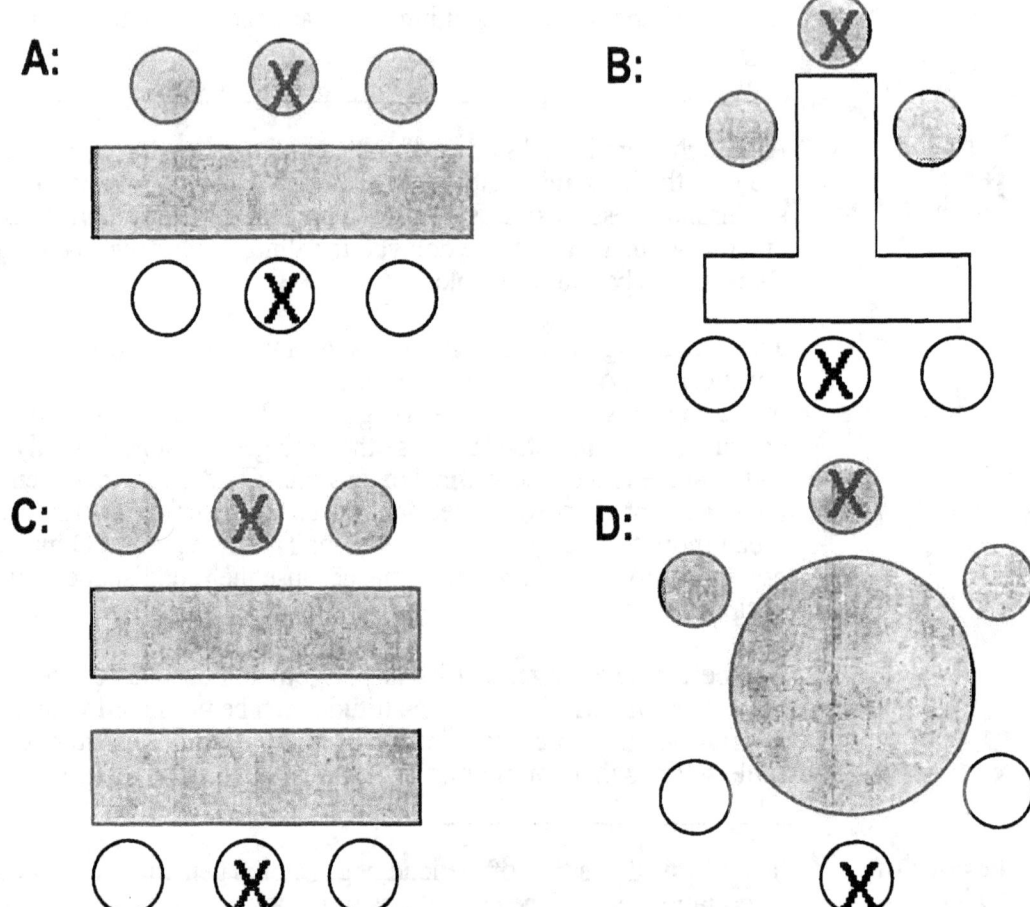

Facility Signals   The facility itself communicates powerful nonverbals. Hosting negotiations in impressive offices at prestige locations conveys positive attributes about the host, such as success and credibility. Conducting negotiation in good facilities can also increase the self-assurance of the host and lower the confidence of the guest negotiators.

Conversely, negotiations held at substandard locations convey nonverbals with unflattering interpretations. Moreover, poor facilities may lower the confidence of the host team while increasing the self-assurance of the guest negotiators. And since many of the facility nonverbals are communicated to the subconscious, bargainers may not even realize the effect on in their confidence levels.

Besides conveying positive or negative attitudes about negotiator confidence, facility nonverbals convey messages about other traits of the host organization, such as quality. For these reasons many restaurants maintain clean restrooms to enhance the perceived quality of their food products.

The nonverbals generated by facility signals are often powerful enough to have a significant influence on negotiations. A Microsoft Corporation executive regained confidence during important negotiations with IBM when he noticed old, outdated computer equipment used in the "Big Blue" offices. The unflattering nonverbal message transmitted by the dated equipment encouraged the executive to stand firm and not to back down in negotiations with the computer giant.

The government side is sometimes at a disadvantage compared to the contractor team in regard to facility nonverbals. This occurs because many contractors often have impressive offices at prestigious locations, while government offices located in older buildings are frequently not as attractive. Nevertheless, the government side can overcome this disadvantage by making the negotiation setting as presentable as possible or selecting better alternative sites. The government team members should also not let unflattering facility nonverbals diminish their own self-confidence or feel a need to apologize for a poor office environment.

7.4 Recognize the Importance of Personal Appearance in Negotiations

Personal Appearance

The value of personal appearance in projecting nonverbals during negotiations cannot be overstated. Since our society attaches so much importance to the way someone looks, numerous conscious and subliminal nonverbals are communicated by dress and appearance. Without question, personal image will influence the negotiation by conveying positive or negative attributes about both the negotiators and their bargaining positions.

Many otherwise good negotiators overlook the importance of personal appearance during negotiations, and consequently lose credibility. The other side may even feel slighted by inappropriate appearance. For example, entering into a negotiation wearing sports clothes may convey a lack of professionalism or even incompetence. Even if the nonverbal message is incorrect, the perception of the other side will be more important than the actual facts.

Make sure your personal appearance is conducive to negotiation success. Appear for negotiations as you would dress for a promotion or job interview. Do not let improper grooming, such as uncombed hair or an unshaven look, detract from your appearance and communicate unfavorable nonverbals about you or your bargaining position. Remember, that if you look good, you will generally feel and perform better.

7.5 Recognize Nonverbal Messages Indicated by the Human Voice and Handshake

Voice Sounds

The nonverbals communicated by the sound of the human voice, known as vocalics, can transmit valuable information during negotiations. This area includes the inflection of the voice, pronunciation of words, the volume of the voice, and the speed of delivery.

The precise way the voice sounds projects positive or negative signals which can influence the negotiations. For example, a harsh or loud delivery could alienate people and indicate a win/lose negotiation style. Similarly, tentativeness in speech could be an indication of uncertainty, while mumbling could even indicate deceit. Likewise, mispronouncing words could imply ignorance or incompetence. And like all nonverbals, the sound of the voice transmits both conscious and subliminal messages.

Government negotiators can use this form of nonverbal communication to their advantage by speaking at a moderate pace in a confident and articulate manner. In this regard, you might need to practice the delivery beforehand and rehearse difficult words or technical statements. Since negotiators are trying to "sell" their position, it is important to speak in a calm, persuasive manner and not to raise your voice or talk harshly. In addition, the government side can obtain useful information from the other side by listening not only to what is said, but how the words are spoken.

The Handshake Most negotiations begin and end with a handshake. The physical clasping of hands indicates nonverbal communication conveyed by touching behavior (haptics). Nonverbal messages are transmitted by the way the handshake feels to each side. And since this communication is frequently conveyed as a subliminal message and has a significant influence on perception, government negotiators should be aware of the importance of the handshake.

Although the handshake concludes most negotiated agreements, the most meaningful handshake generally occurs at the start of the negotiations when the government and contractor teams are introduced to each other. This initial handshake conveys an important first impression to each side even when the participants are not consciously aware of the nonverbal message.

A firm handshake or "executive grip" conveys such positive attributes as power, confidence, and sincerity. In contrast, a loose handshake may send unflattering messages of weakness and insecurity. Some people may even feel slighted when someone uses a casual handshake or just grasps their fingertips. The positive signals conveyed by an appropriate handshake should be accompanied, and thereby reinforced, by other forms of consistent nonverbal messages. For example, handshakers should smile and look the other person straight in the eye to signal honesty and friendliness. Handshakes concluding an agreement could be accomplished by prolonging the shake, by using both hands, or by extending the other hand on the shoulder or upper arm of the other party. Using the other hand in such ways often represents higher degrees of agreement.

Government bargainers can often enhance their images with proper handshakes. Although the nonverbals communicated by the handshake may only represent perceptions to the subconscious mind, the perception of each side is often more important than the actual facts.

7.6 Summary

Summary

Bargainers need an understanding of the different forms of nonverbal communicating to increase the likelihood of successful negotiations. An awareness of nonverbals can be used to obtain important information from the other side. Since nonverbals tend to be more honest than verbal communication, the two types of messages can be compared to detect deception. Negotiators can also use nonverbals to strengthen their bargaining position and avoid unintentional signals that are detrimental to their side. Government bargainers, the people in general, cannot avoid communicating with nonverbals because this form of communication comes naturally. The only question is whether the nonverbal messages sent and received will either help or hinder our ability to negotiate successfully.

CHAPTER 8: COMPETITIVE DISCUSSIONS

Learning Objectives

At the end of this chapter you will be able to:

Primary Learning Objective (PLO)
Conduct competitive discussions.

Classroom Learning Objective 8/1
Describe fundamental differences between the bargaining environments in competitive and sole source procurements.

Classroom Learning Objective 8/2
Identify the distinguishing characteristics of the competitive discussions process.

Classroom Learning Objective 8/3
Identify the steps in conducting competitive discussion process.

Classroom Learning Objective 8/4
Apply the special rules for competitive discussions.

Contents and Procedures

Procedures   The following flowchart shows the steps in competitive negotiation:

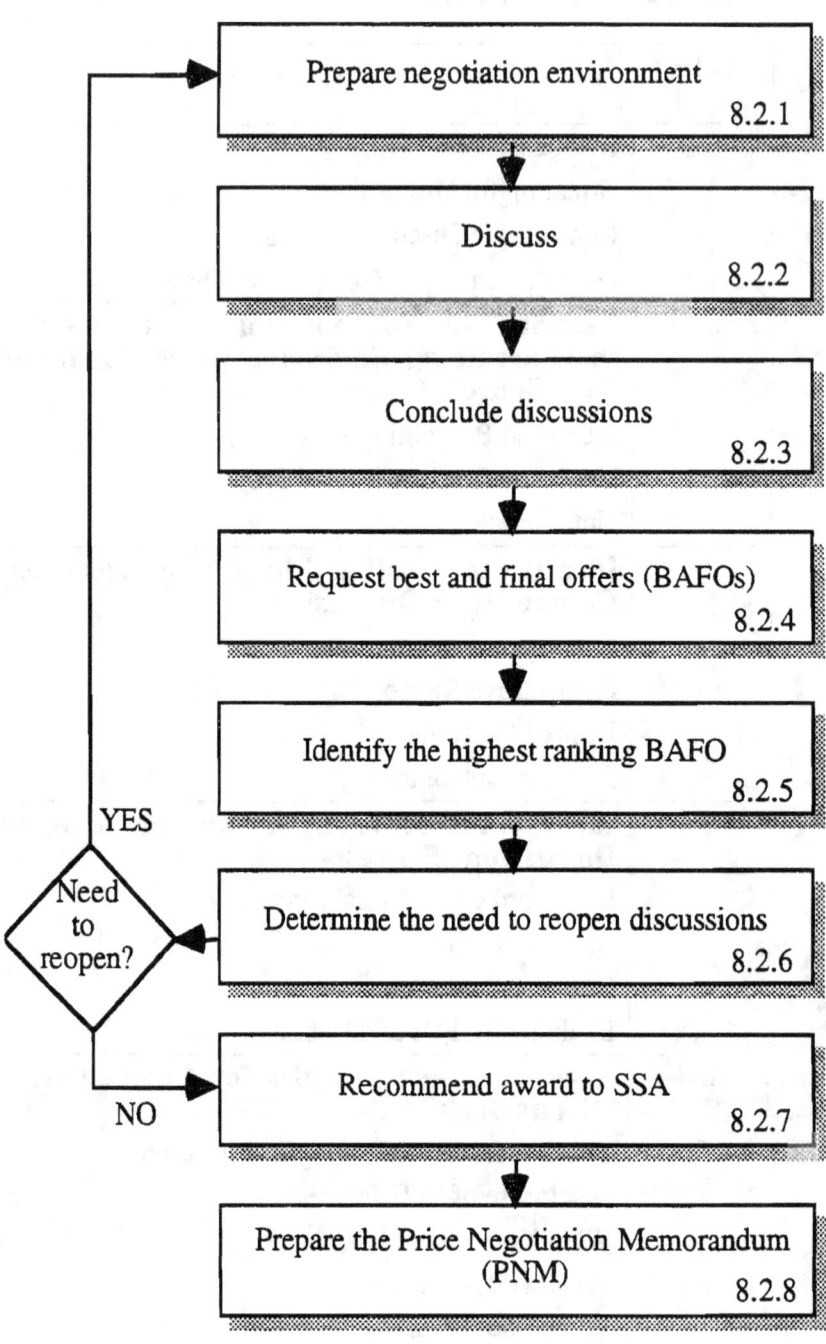

8.0 Introduction

"Meaningful Discussions"

Competitive discussions enhance competition by allowing negotiations with multiple offerors who submit differing proposals. Before selecting the winning source or contractor, the government can hold "meaningful discussions" with those offerors falling within a competitive range. This process, known as the "conduct of meaningful discussions," allows the government side to bring out proposal weaknesses and deficiencies so offerors can make improvements before submitting a best and final offer (BAFO).

Competitive Discussion Defined

The FAR defines "discussion" as including any oral or written communication between the government and an offeror, other than communications only for the purpose of minor clarification. All discussions are accomplished in private communication between each offeror and the government that:

- Involve information essential for determining the acceptability of a proposal or
- Provide the offeror an opportunity to revise or modify its proposal.

Although competitive discussions are more restrictive than typical sole source negotiations in that certain information cannot be disclosed, the "discussions" addressed in this chapter are a form of contract negotiations used when the government bargains with more than one contractor.

Overall Purpose of Competitive Discussions

Since each proposal offers distinct supplies or services, discussions are needed to determine which proposal will best fill the government requirement.

8.1 Describe the Fundamental Differences Between the Bargaining Environments of Competitive and Sole Source Procurements

Increased Bargaining Power

The primary difference in the bargaining environment of competitive discussions compared to sole source negotiations is the greater bargaining power possessed by the government side. In sole source negotiations, the contractor side has the bargaining advantage because the government needs the unique deliverable provided by the single source. In competitive discussions, this bargaining power is heavily on the government side by virtue of the competition between offerors.

Unreasonably Low Priced Proposals

Since the bargaining power more decidedly favors the government, offerors are sometimes tempted to submit unrealistically low prices to win contract award. This is especially true in competitions for cost-type contracts (see FAR 15.605(d). Under cost plus fixed fee contracts, there is essentially no penalty for underestimating costs since the contractor is reimbursed for all allowable costs. For fixed price contracts, "buy-in" contractors may try to recoup their losses with high-priced modifications or less than satisfactory output. **In short, the government side should always be alert for extremely low price proposals that are unlikely to satisfy the requirements of the contract.**

Unfavorable Aspects

The favorable bargaining power also tempts the government side to exploit the situation with win/lose tactics, such as auctioning and technical leveling. These tactics are often used in negotiations outside the government where a firm negotiates the best deal and then tells competitors to submit even lower prices. Because of the enhanced bargaining position and resulting temptation, the FAR established special rules to observe during competitive discussions which are not applicable to sole source negotiations.

Finally, the increased competition inherent in competitive discussion sometimes tempts offerors to use unsavory methods to win the contract. These negative ramifications include temptations to illicitly obtain information on competing proposals. Some offerors may also be tempted to collude with other offerors to eliminate the effect of the competition.

8.2 Identify the Distinguishing Characteristics of the Competitive Discussions

Evaluation Factors

In competitive discussions contract price is often less important than other evaluation criteria. Total contract cost is generally only one of several factors used in the Request for Proposal (RFP) to determine the best source. The non-price evaluation factors used to select the best source include:

• Technical Evaluation

The technical evaluation of the proposals is generally conducted by specialists in the area, such as scientific and engineering personnel. This written evaluation includes a narrative on the technical strengths and weaknesses of each proposal and explains determinations of unacceptability.

• Business and Management Evaluation

Management capabilities are appraised using the following factors:

- Management organization
- Availability of required facilities
- Cost controls
- Ability to maintain and account for government furnished property
- Offeror willingness to devote resources to the proposed work

• Past Performance

- Government experience with the offeror
- Private sector experience with the offeror
- History of meeting delivery schedules.
- Other pertinent administrative and business information that may have been requested in the solicitation

Competitive Range

A competitive range is established once all proposals have been rated according to the evaluation criteria stated in the RFP. The competitive range shall include all proposals which have a reasonable chance for award once discussions are held. This determination is extremely important because the government must hold discussions with all offerors falling within the competitive range.

Desired Outcome

In contrast to noncompetitive negotiations where mutual agreement is the desired conclusion, competitive discussions do not end in a deal. Instead, offerors are only encouraged to submit their best and final offers (BAFOs). The government side then evaluates the competing BAFOs and selects the successful proposal after considering all the evaluation factors.

Possible Outcomes

Instead of attempting to reach mutual agreement and finalize a deal, the primary goal of the government in competitive discussions is to *persuade* each offeror to submit a BAFO that represents an improvement over the earlier proposal. The government hopes any revisions will more likely satisfy the government requirements of the proposal and be closer in price to what the government sidebelieves is fair and reasonable.

However, offerors are free to remove themselves from consideration, make no changes at all in their BAFO, or make changes that have no relationship whatsoever to the discussions. On the other hand, there is nothing to prevent the government from obtaining informal agreement on contract terms and conditions with the expectation that the BAFO will reflect the results of the discussion.

8.3 Identify the Steps in Conducting Competitive Discussion Process

Safeguard Confidential Information

The physical environment for competitive discussions is essentially the same as the environment for sole source negotiations with the major exception of increased security considerations. While it is always wise to safeguard confidential information, this practice is imperative when holding competitive discussions. By safeguarding information the government can ensure that offerors do not get an unfair advantage by having access to unauthorized information, such as other proposals or confidential government evaluations. Meetings should also be scheduled in ways to avoid inappropriate contact between competing offerors.

Brief Government Team

Government negotiators should be careful to set the proper tone when entering into competitive negotiations. Immediately prior to the discussions, the chief negotiator should brief the team on the unique nature of the upcoming negotiations. Besides refreshing the team on the protocol discussed in Chapter 4, the briefing should spell out the differences between competitive discussions and other forms of negotiations. **In particular, the government team should be reminded that they may not disclose information that could lead to technical leveling, technical transfusion, or auctioning.** (These differences will be discussed in greater detail later in this chapter.)

Conduct Discussions

The content and extent of discussions with each offeror will be determined by the individual characteristics of each proposal. The contracting officer is required to:

- Attempt to resolve uncertainties concerning the technical aspects or other terms of the proposal. However, suspected mistakes should be identified without revealing information about another proposal.

- Advise each offeror of proposal deficiencies, to provide them with an opportunity to satisfy the government requirements.

- At the conclusion of the discussions, give all offerors still within the competitive range the opportunity to submit a BAFO by providing them a common cut-off date for revising their proposals.

Evaluate BAFOs and Debrief

Once BAFOs are received, final step in the competitive discussion process is the evaluation of all BAFOs to determine which offeror to recommend to the source selection authority (SSA). The SSA then has the ultimate authority to decide on which proposal will win the contract. Following notice of award, the losing offerors may request a debriefing on why the winning proposal was selected.

8.4 Apply the Special Rules for Competitive Discussions

The Concept of "Meaningful Discussions"

Before entering into competitive discussions, the government side should develop separate negotiation positions for each proposal. How you persuade an offeror to improve a proposal is different than in noncompetitive negotiations because of the Comptroller General (GAO) requirement that discussions be "meaningful". To conduct meaningful discussions, the government side must disclose deficiencies, uncertainties, or mistakes, and provide an opportunity for the offeror to revise the proposal. In the true win/win spirit, the government side may also want to acknowledge some of the positive aspects of a proposal.

Remember, all offerors with whom you hold discussions must be provided an opportunity to submit a "best and final offer" but it is up to each offeror to determine if and how the offer should be modified.

Disclosure of Deficiencies

A deficiency is any part of a proposal that fails to satisfy the government requirements. Deficiencies should be derived only from the evaluation of each proposal against the specific evaluation criteria or the minimum requirements in the solicitation. **In no event are deficiencies to be derived from a comparative evaluation of the relative strengths and weaknesses of different proposals.** Deficiencies include such matters as:

- Unrealistic cost estimates,
- Failures to meet specifications,
- Failures to submit required information, or
- Questionable technical or management approaches.

Some guidelines follow:

- The content and extent of discussion is a matter of the contracting officer's judgment based on the particular facts of the procurement. In this regard, treat discussions with each offeror as a sole source negotiation on the merits of that offeror's proposal.

- You are under no obligation to discuss every aspect of the proposal. Instead, you are required only to reasonably lead offerors into those areas of their proposals considered deficient within the context of the procurement.

- Government must be as specific as possible in its communication. An offeror should not be left with the impression that there are no remaining deficient areas when deficiencies still exist.

- Discussions with an offeror should be confined only to a specific proposal and its related deficiencies. Do not engage in technical transfusion by avoiding the disclosure of the strengths and weaknesses of competing offerors, or revealing technical information, ideas, or cost data from another proposal.

What You Cannot Do

In competitive discussions, you cannot:

• Use auction techniques, such as:

  - Indicating to an offeror a cost or price that it must meet to obtain further consideration,
  - Advising an offeror of its price standing relative to another offeror (however, it is permissible to inform an offeror that its price is considered by the government to be too high or unrealistic), and
  - Otherwise furnishing information about other offeror's prices.

• Engage in technical transfusion — disclosing technical information provided by one offeror to another offeror, resulting in improvements to the second offeror's proposal.

• Engage in technical leveling—helping an offeror to bring its proposal up to the level of other proposals by repeatedly pointing out or explaining technical weaknesses.

• Otherwise tell one offeror about the proposals of other competitors since such action would give an unfair advantage to some firms and would invite protests.

What You Must Do

In competitive discussions, you must:

• Treat all offerors the same.

• Attempt to resolve any uncertainties concerning the technical proposal and other terms and conditions of the proposal, especially those that would have an impact on price.

• Advise the offeror of reasons for believing that the price is unreasonably high based on data from the offeror or comparisons with historical prices, commercial prices, and other estimates (but not the price proposed by other offerors).

• Identify suspected pricing mistakes by bringing them to the offeror's attention as specifically as possible without disclosing information on prices or evaluations of other proposals. This is especially important when the proposed price appears to be a "buy-in" and is so far below your minimum position as to not be considered fair and reasonable.

• Provide the offeror a reasonable opportunity to submit any pricing, technical, or other revisions to its proposal that may result from the discussions.

What You Can Do   In competitive discussions, you can also:

- Point out any proposal variation from the RFP that you believe is unnecessary and may have affected the proposed price.

- Discuss potential tradeoffs between price and other contract terms.

- Point to indicators that the proposed price is too high, such as the producer price index, historical or commercial prices, and cost estimating relationships.

- Ask the offeror to "sharpen its pencils" or otherwise urge the offeror to improve on price in the BAFO – especially when coupled with a persuasive presentation of facts and reasoning supporting your contention that the offeror could do better on price.

- Present a position on price and the rationale for that price. The Comptroller General[1] ruled that contracting officers can:

  - Develop a separate negotiation price objective for each proposal based on a separate appraisal of that proposal

  - Disclose that objective to the offeror as a negotiation tool for reaching an agreement as to a fair and reasonable price.

- Obtain informal agreement on terms and conditions with the expectation that the BAFO will reflect the results of the discussion.

---

[1] In the matter of Racal Guardata, Inc. (B-245139.2, February 7, 1992), the contracting officer asked one offeror to reduce its price by 10 percent and another by 30 percent. The Comptroller General did not consider this to be "a prohibited auction" since the Government's price objective for each offeror was based on a comparison of the proposed price with catalog prices and prior contract prices – not with other offered prices.

8.5 Summary

Summary

Competitive discussions is a form of negotiation where the government conducts discussions with multiple offerors who submit differing proposals. In this type of negotiation, price is often less important than the technical evaluation and other criteria. Instead of attempting to reach mutual agreement, the desired outcome of competitive discussions is to persuade each offeror to submit a BAFO that represents an improvement of their earlier proposal.

Because of the increased bargaining power resulting from the competitive nature of this form of negotiation, the government side is bound by special rules. In particular, the government side is prohibited from engaging in auction techniques, technical leveling, technical transfusion, or otherwise telling one offeror about competitive proposals. In short, the government is required to treat all offerors fairly and equally.

www.ingramcontent.com/pod-product-compliance
Lightning Source LLC
Chambersburg PA
CBHW081153180526

45170CB00006B/2064